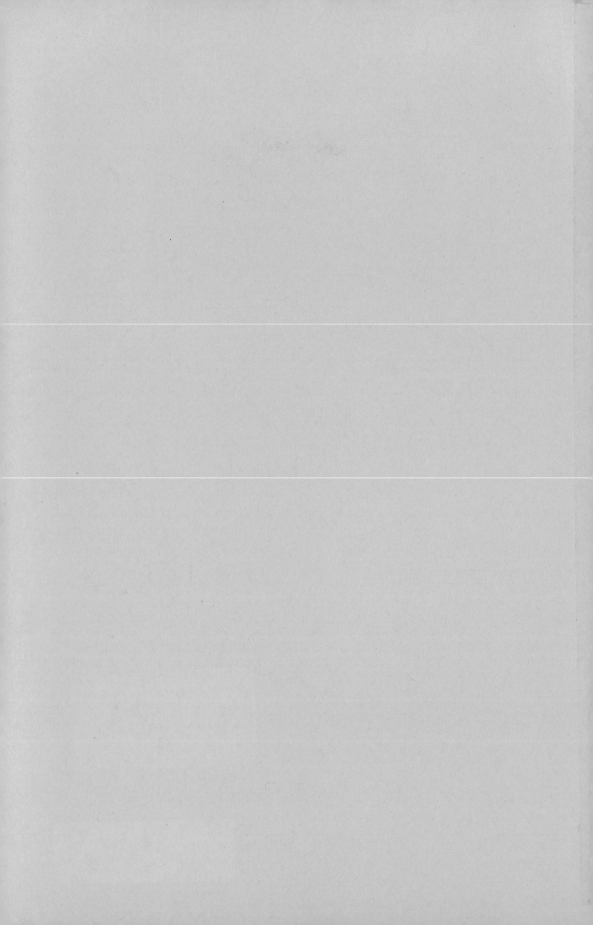

Process Improvement and Organizational Learning:

The Role of Collaboration Technologies

Ned Kock
Temple University

IDEA GROUP PUBLISHING
Hershey USA • London UK

Senior Editor:	Mehdi Khosrowpour
Managing Editor:	Jan Travers
Copy Editor:	John Syphrit
Typesetter:	Tamara Gillis
Cover Design:	Marjaneh Talebi
Printed at:	BookCrafters

Published in the United States of America by
   Idea Group Publishing
   1331 E. Chocolate Avenue
   Hershey PA 17033-1117
   Tel: 717-533-8845
   Fax: 717-533-8661
   E-mail: jtravers@idea-group.com
   Website: http://www.idea-group.com

and in the United Kingdom by
   Idea Group Publishing
   3 Henrietta Street
   Covent Garden
   London WC2E 8LU
   Tel: 171-240 0856
   Fax: 171-379 0609
   Website: http://www.eurospan.co.uk

Library of Congress Cataloging-in-Publication Data

Kock, Ned, 1964-
       Process improvement and organizational learning: the role of collaboration technologies/Ned Kock.
             p. cm.
       Includes bibliographical references and index.
       ISBN 1-878289-58-6 (pbk.)
1. Organizational learning. 2. Reengineering (Management)
I. Title.
HD58.82.K63 1999   98-51559
658.4'063--dc21   CIP

British Cataloguing in Publication Data
A Cataloguing in Publication record for this book is available from the British Library.

Other IDEA GROUP Publishing Books

- Measuring IT Investment Payoff/Mahmood/Szewczak 1-878289-42-X
- IT Diffusion in the Asia Pacific/Tan/Corbett/Wong 1-878289-8-9
- Information Technology and Computer Applications in Public Administration/Garson 1-878289-52-7
- Telelearning via the Internet/Kouki/Wright 1-878289-53-5
- IS Innovation and Diffusion: Issues and Directions/Larsen and McGuire 1-878289-43-8
- The Virtual Workplace/Igbaria and Tan 1-878289-41-1
- Information Systems Success Measurement /Garrity/ Sanders 1-878289-44-6
- Cases on IT Management in Modern Organizations/Liebowitz/Khosrowpour 1-878289-37-3
- Business Process Change: Reengineering Concepts, Methods and Technologies/Grover/ Kettinger 1-878289-29-2
- Cleanroom Software Engineering Practices/Becker/Whittaker 1-878289-34-9
- Collaborative Technologies and Organizational Learning/Neilson 1-878289-39-X
- Computer-Aided Software Engineering: Issues and Trends for the 1990s and Beyond/ Bergin 1-878289-15-2
- Computer Technology and Social Issues/Garson 1-878289-28-4
- Emerging Information Technologies for Competitive Advantage and Economic Development 1-878289-17-9
- Global Info. Infrastructure:The Birth, Vision and Architecture/Targowski 1-878289-32-2
- Global Issues of Information Technology Management/ Palvia/Palvia/Zigli 1-878289-10-1
- Global Information Systems and Technology: Focus on the Organization and Its Functional Areas/Deans/Karwan 1-878289-21-7
- Global Information Technology Education: Issues and Trends/Khosrowpour/Loch 1-878289-14-4
- The Human Side of Information Technology Management/ Szewczak/Khosrowpour 1-878289-33-0
- Information Systems Outsourcing Decision Making: A Managerial Approach/de Looff 1-878289-40-3
- Information Technology and Organizations: Challenges of New Technologies/ Khosrowpour 1-878289-18-7
- IT Management and Organizational Innovations 1-878289-35-7
- Managing Information & Communications in a Changing Global Environment 1-878289-31-4
- Managing Social and Economic Change With Information Technology/Khosrowpour 1-878289-26-8
- Management Impacts of Information Technology/ Szewczak/ Snodgrass/Khosrowpour 1-878289-08-X
- Managing Expert Systems /Turban/Liebowitz 1-878289-11-X
- Managing Information Technology in a Global Society/Khosrowpour 1-878289-13-6
- Managing Microcomputer Technology as an Organizational Resource /Khosrowpour/ Amoroso 1-878289-07-1
- Managing Information Resources in the 1990s 1-878289-06-3
- Multimedia Computing: Preparing for the 21st Century/Reisman 1-878289-22-5
- Partners Not Competitors: The Age of Teamwork and Technology/Oliva 1-878289-09-8
- Reengineering MIS: Aligning Information Technology and Business Operations/Coleman 1-878289-30-6
- Strategic Management: An Integrative Context-Specific Process/Mockler 1-878289-19-5

Excellent additions to your library!

Process Improvement and Organizational Learning: The Role of Collaboration Technologies

Table of Contents

Preface

This book has been written around two main theses. The first is that process improvement, a key element of the most influential management movements in the 1980s and 1990s, can be itself considerably improved by the use of information technology. I argue that distributed and asynchronous group support systems; such as e-mail, computer conferencing and the World Wide Web, are likely to play a major role in this improvement.

The second thesis put forth by this book is that process improvement affects organizational learning in a non-linear way, and that the use of information technology can boost this influence by increasing the breadth and speed of knowledge dissemination in organizations. To lay the ground for this, I explore the relationship between the concepts of data, information and knowledge. I do so by looking at how these abstract entities affect our lives. These concepts are then used as the building blocks to define organizational cognition and, more specifically, organizational learning.

The relationship between collaborative technologies, process improvement, and organizational learning is analyzed in this book. I base my investigation on my experience in more than 15 process-focused organizational development projects, and a three-year project where over 38 process improvement groups were facilitated with the support of collaborative technologies. Finally, I analyze critical success factors in distributed computer-supported process improvement groups.

My goal with this book is to help managers, as well as students who are pursuing a management career, to prepare their (future and present) organizations to survive and thrive in the information era. In such era the fittest organizations are those able to master the art of efficient and effective acquisition and use of data, information and knowledge.

The contents of this book

This book is made up of seven chapters and two appendices, grouped in two parts—Part I and Part II. The content presented in the seven chapters flows so as to introduce the reader to fundamental ideas, develop and support with evidence the two basic theses of this book, and finally offer some advice to organizations on how to implement them.

Chapter 1 offers a historical review of the fields of organizational development and collaborative computing. This review focuses on major historical events, and does not restrict itself to academic issues. As such, several of the major management developments are discussed, from Adam Smith's division of labor approach in the 1700s to Hammer and Champy's reengineering movement in the 1990s. Subsequently, the chapter describes the main technological developments that led to the emergence of collaborative computing as a significant tool for organizational improvement and learning. I try in this chapter to build a link between the commercial establishment of computing technologies and the organizational development ideas that became popular at the same period. This should help readers to understand how technology has evolved together with management ideas, and get situated in the topical discussion in further chapters.

In spite of the recent popularity that the business process concept has gained, I believe it to be a fundamental idea behind several management movements, including the total quality management, organizational learning, and business process reengineering movements. Therefore, I thought I should use a full chapter to discuss the concept. I did so in Chapter 2, where I discuss process in the context of the management movements just mentioned. I also describe several popular views of processes, with particular attention to the data and workflow views.

Chapter 3 is also an introductory chapter. It discusses three fundamental concepts referred to throughout the book—data, information and knowledge. This chapter is particularly important because of the rather confuse way in which these terms are used in both academic as well as more popular senses. There I offer new conceptualizations that suggest that data are carriers of information and knowledge, as well as that while information is eminently descriptive, knowledge is mostly predictive in nature. Although these conceptualizations are heavily based on previous theoretical frameworks from cognitive science and artificial intelligence, I tried to eliminate technical jargon as much as possible and explain my views through examples involving simple day-to-day situations.

Chapter 4 is the last chapter in Part I of this book, even though it presents and discusses empirical evidence that supports one of the theses of this book —that process improvement affects organizational learning in a non-linear way. The reason this chapter is in Part I is because it does not discuss any direct effect that technology has on people. It rather targets a specific group process, the process improvement process, and shows that this group process per se leads to increased knowledge communication and sharing in organizations.

An extensive discussion of the direct and indirect effects that collaborative technologies are likely to have on process improvement and organizational learning is provided in Chapter 5. This is one of the core chapters of the book, the first of Part II, and addresses both of the two main theses of this book. Most of the chapter is about technology effects regarding process improvement. The emphasis is on asynchronous technologies, particularly those based on the electronic mail paradigm. At the end of the chapter, a discussion about the impact on organizational learning is presented. This discussion builds on evidence presented in Chapter 4.

While Chapter 5 suggests an overall positive impact of collaborative technologies on process improvement and organizational learning, it does not address success factors related to computer support improvement and learning groups. This situation is corrected in Chapter 6, where a careful analysis of 12 groups leads to the identification of a few critical success factors. This chapter discusses the appropriateness of computer support in incremental and radical improvement situations, and shows that computer support can become a trap to organizations if not properly employed.

Chapter 7 summarizes the findings discussed in previous chapters, particularly those in Chapter 5. This is done through a causal model depicting an integrated view of computer support effects on distributed process improvement groups and organizational learning. This chapter also presents a number of "realistic" recommendations for organizations, trying to avoid much of the self-servicing advice seen in popular business publications.

Two appendices are provided at the end of the book. Appendix A is a detailed description of MetaProi, the group methodology I used to facilitate the groups I studied for this book. I expect this appendix to be instrumental in similar future initiatives by the readers of this book. Appendix B provides a summarized and structured description of 12 cases of computer-supported process improvement and learning. As these cases served as the basis for several of the ideas in the book, I think they will be useful to readers who want to draw their own conclusions based on raw data.

Acknowledgments
I should first thank my family. They have learned how to live with someone who is openly a workaholic, and who spends of a lot of time staring at books and computer screens. Yet, they know that I love them with all my heart.

This book has its roots in my Ph.D. project, and therefore benefited directly and indirectly from all those with whom I interacted as a doctoral student. My special thanks go to my Ph.D. advisor, Bob McQueen, and his family. Bob has not only provided excellent academic support throughout my Ph.D. research, but also sincere friendship and advice about general life matters. He and his wife, Anita McQueen have gone out of their way to make me feel as comfortable and at home as possible.

I would like to acknowledge the invaluable cooperation of the organizations investigated in this book. Among their employees, Peter Grace, Robert Wellington and Andrea Jenkins deserve a special mention, for their ideas and help in the collection of empirical evidence.

Many thanks to the School of Management Studies at the University of Waikato, and in particular of the Department of Management Systems, for their constant support and for providing a stimulating research and academic environment.

Finally, I would like to thank the many friends I have made in New Zealand for their hospitality and the wonderful time we spent together.

Ned Kock
Philadelphia
October 18, 1998

Part I

Process Improvement and Organizational Learning

Chapter 1

Introduction

A historic view of organizational development

Organizational development is the generic field of research and practice concerned with structural organizational changes that can have a positive impact on competitiveness. It is about changing organizations in order to make them more competitive, chiefly through modifications in organizational *structure*. Historically, most organizational development efforts have aimed at improving productivity (e.g. cycle time and cost reduction) and quality (e.g. boosting customer satisfaction). Organizational development encompasses procedural and policy changes within firms in order to adapt to external factors. External factors include competitive pressures, as well as economic and government regulation changes.

The history of organizational development is closely linked with the history of management. Those who have initiated and championed organizational development projects typically have also had the responsibility of coordinating the efficient and effective deployment of human and material resources in organizations as managers, management consultants, or action-oriented management researchers.

Although the development of management as an academic discipline is a relatively recent one, management procedures that resemble those commonly used today in large corporations can be traced back to as early as 5,000 BC. At that time, the Sumerians had developed careful record-keeping procedures. The Egyptians followed, with the development of planning and coordination procedures that are reflected in the precision with which they have accomplished a number of very complex undertakings, such as the large irrigation networks build around the Nile River and the Great Pyramids.

The expansion of the Roman Empire and the need to effectively manage occupied territories and provinces has seen the development of common measurement systems and standards to facilitate communication. This period has also seen the development of job descriptions to ensure that people in management and administrative roles clearly understood what was expected from them.

Italian merchants have developed elaborate bookkeeping procedures in the Middle Ages. These included the introduction of the double-entry (debit-credit) bookkeeping approach by the Franciscan priest Luca Pacioli, the basics of costs accounting, and concepts of journal entries and ledgers. At the same period, the benefits of task specialization (which preceded the concept of division of labor) and rudiments of strategic management have been proposed by Thomas More in England, and Niccolo Machiavelli in Italy.

Adam Smith, a professor at Glasgow University, in Scotland, later picked up the theme of task specialization and became famous for his investigations of its impact on manufacturing activities. Among other things, he showed that manifold gains in productivity could be achieved in manufacturing activities if every worker focused their efforts on one simple task of an assembly line (Smith, 1910; 1910a). This set the stage for the division of labor seen throughout the Industrial Revolution.

Smith's theories, in turn, influenced Eli Whitney, who pioneered the practical implementation of mass production in the late 1790s, in the United States. Whitney and Simeon North applied mass production techniques to the manufacture of guns, for which they secured large multi-year government contracts. At about the same time in England, James Watt and Matthew Robinson Boulton have developed the concepts of standard operating procedures, production cells, and incentive payments.

The Industrial Era

His contributions to manufacturing management notwithstanding, James Watt is probably better known for having perfected the steam engine (whose patent was granted to him in 1769) and thus paving the way for the First Industrial Revolution (generally seen as the period from around 1770 to 1850). The First Industrial Revolution produced managerial challenges that were previously unthinkable. New manufacturing techniques drove a tremendous expansion in the markets for machines built around steam engine principles. Steam ships and locomotives were developed, which led to a tremendous growth in canal and road transport, and, in turn, in trade in general. These gave rise to a number of new management problems and situations, as well as opportunities for organizational development.

The two main management figures of the First Industrial Revolution were Henry Fayol and Frederick Winslow Taylor. Fayol pioneered what became known as "functionalism" — a set of prescriptions to structure large organizations around forecasting, planning, and coordination activities. Later, functionalism was successfully put into practice by Alfred P. Sloan at General Motors. But the giant of this period was undoubtedly Taylor, whose principles of scientific management (Taylor, 1911) had an impact that extended well beyond his time.

Taylor, who was born in Germantown, Pennsylvania, was perhaps one of the first true organizational development consultants. He believed in continuous improvement through the careful and precise measurement of the times and motions involved in relatively simple manufacturing activities. After having worked in several different positions at a company called Midvale Steel Works and started up his own new capitalist venture, Taylor took on a management consulting career with the publication of the best-selling book *A Piece Rate System* (Taylor, 1885). In spite of its strong dehumanization element, which led to strong union opposition, Taylor's system still lives on to some extent, particularly in organizational development approaches focused on increasing *productivity* (and without a direct concern with *quality*).

Taylor's antithesis, in management conviction terms, was Elton Mayo, a social psychologist born in Adelaide, Australia. Mayo's contribution significance lies in his ideas about the importance of non-economic rewards and personal satisfaction to employee productivity. His criticism of the model proposed by Taylor was rooted in the fact that it devised optimal work procedures and imposed them on the workers, through a system of simple financial incentives, without giving workers the opportunity to provide their input. Mayo provided scientific evidence that taking workers' attitudes and personal motivations into consideration when designing work paid off in economic terms. He investigated the relationships between people working together and, unlike Taylor, paid relatively little attention to such things as procedural routines, times, and motions. What both Taylor and Mayo shared, however, was their main goal, which was the improvement of organizations.

Mayo's most important research project was labeled the Hawthorne Investigations. It was a ten-year project conducted at Western Electric Company's Hawthorne Works in Chicago. The project began in 1927 and involved around 20,000 subjects and 100 investigators. Its main focus was the behavior of small groups under different physical working configurations and social stimuli. Among its main findings was the notion that, for the average worker, the desire to stand well with one's fellows easily outweighs the influence of financial rewards and physical working conditions.

The world was well into the Second Industrial Revolution, a period that goes from approximately 1850 to the years preceding the official start of World War II, when Mayo's studies began. This period has seen many successful organizational development practitioners, from which some were full time executives at large companies that later became landmarks in the history of corporate US. Among these are Henry Ford I and Alfred P. Sloan.

Henry Ford I, founder of Ford Motor Company, is viewed by many as the inventor of the automotive assembly line as well as the first to use mass assembly line production as a means to successfully compete based on price. Alfred P. Sloan, an MIT-trained engineer and former president of General Motors, is credited with the development and practical implementation of the concept of "multi-division company." He implemented this concept by breaking up General Motors into a set of independent divisions (each with its own engineering, production and sales departments), all of which reporting to a corporate control division comprising mostly top management personnel[1].

The Post-War Era

The Industrial Era was marked by an organizational development focus on autocratic and control-centered approaches, which placed emphasis on managers rather than employees. Even Mayo, who added a more humanistic view to the problem of making organizations more productive, has been criticized by what some viewed as an *objectification* of human beings. While he recognized that the workers' organizational beliefs and motivations where important determinants of productivity, some accused him of blindly adhering to the industry's own view of employees as means to be manipulated or adjusted to impersonal ends.

After World War II, in the period that I generally refer to here as the Post-War Era (from the end of the war to the late 1980s), some influential management thinkers embraced the management-centered view of organizational development that was prevalent in the Industrial Era. One such thinker was Douglas McGregor, who argued that the basic beliefs held by managers deeply influence the inner workings of organizations. This general hypothesis framed the development of McGregor's hierarchy of needs, and his two theories of how management behavior shapes organizations. These theories became known as Theory X, which refers to autocratic managers, and Theory Y, which refers to managers who delegate responsibilities to workers. These two theories were, according to McGregor, two extremes of a continuum that were not usually found in organizations in their pure form.

Nevertheless, a former collaborator of McGregor, psychologist Abraham Maslow, became a strong champion of the implementation of Theory Y in organizations, combining it with a refined version of McGregor's hierarchy of needs. By adopting Theory Y, organizations would benefit from what Maslow saw as an inherent characteristic of human beings—a deep-rooted need to work. Although Maslow's idealistic strain has been strongly criticized, it provided a welcome shift from the organizational structure-centered themes that dominated organizational development thinking in the Industrial Era.

A contemporary of Maslow, clinical psychologist turned organizational development consultant Frederick Herzberg, was another nonconformist of this period. He developed a theory of organizational work that separated stimulating factors in the workplace into two main categories— *hygiene* and *motivation* factors. According to Herzberg's theory, both types of factors must be satisfied if optimum productivity and quality is to be achieved. Hygiene factors are related to the satisfaction of basic animal needs, such as the need for nourishment and health care. Motivation factors are related to the satisfaction of social and intellectual needs, such as the need to be liked by others. Herzberg theories are seen as the basis for many contemporary job enrichment approaches, such as flextime (i.e. allowing workers to take on flexible time schedules) and several different worker compensation schemes.

The Post-War era also saw the emergence of two of what were later to become very influential approaches for organizational development—action learning and organizational learning. Action learning was pioneered by Reg Revans, who argued that small groups of peers, from factory floor workers to managers, could learn from and support each other so as to achieve significant gains in productivity and quality. Revans insisted that only those who are directly involved in doing the work can effectively improve it, an idea that is at the roots of the development of "quality circles" in Japan. Chris Argyris, who criticized formal organizational systems stemming from the scientific management movement for neglecting both the social and egotistical needs of individuals, pioneered the concept of organizational learning, one of the main topics of this book. Argyris introduced important concepts, such as those of single-loop and double-loop learning, and worked closely with Donald Schon. Single-loop learning is predominantly reactive and attempts to maintain the status quo, no matter how bad it is. Double-loop learning is proactive, and is aimed at changing the structures and paradigms that underlie well established yet unproductive work practices. Argyris and Schon published several books together, including *Organizational Learning*, in 1978 (Argyris and Schon, 1978).

The Post-War era also provided a nurturing environment for the birth and growth of the quality movement. The two principal figures of this movement were William E. Deming, a statistician with a PhD in physics, and Joseph M. Juran, a former engineer at American Telephone and Telegraph (AT&T).

Deming was one of the first to suggest a shift from problems to *processes* as the focus of organizational development, and was highly respected in Japan as an organizational consultant. Deming, who argued for process-focused improvement methods that emphasized the use of statistics, is credited with part of the economic turnaround that happened in Japan from 1950 to 1980. According to him, all processes are subject to a certain degree of variability, which can reduce the quality of the process outputs. If this degree of variability is reduced, average quality will increase as a result. Deming also extended Pareto's rule to management, by arguing that only 15 percent of manufacturing problems are caused by workers, while 85 percent of those problems are caused by process design and management.

Like Deming, Juran had worked as an organizational development consultant in Japan in the years that followed the end of World War II. He had, however, taken a different approach than Deming's, focusing mostly on top management practices for ensuring quality. Juran has suggested that Deming was more comfortable with statistics than with management issues, and that what were often seen as visionary statements were little more than far-out statements and platitudes that, as many other management ideas, gained acceptance by being repeated over and over again. Still, some believe that Juran's influence on organizational development thinking has been a minor one if compared with Deming's, who many view as the father of what later became known as the total quality management (TQM) movement.

Finally, one more influential movement whose peak occurred in the 1980s was the "excellence" movement. The most popular writers of this movement are undoubtedly Tom Peters and Robert Waterman, whose best-seller *In Search of Excellence* sold over five million copies worldwide (Peters and Waterman, 1982). It is difficult to single out a set of major ideas that emerged from the early excellence movement pioneered by Peters and Waterman, which was seen as a group of disconnected practices by successful companies conveyed in a very simplified (maybe oversimplified) and optimistic way. One of Peters' subsequent books, *Passion for Excellence*, introduced the concept of "management by walking around" (MBWA), which also enjoyed some popularity. Another contributor to the excellence movement was Rosabeth Moss Kanter, a respected scholar in her own right, whose book *The Change Masters* was hailed as the thinking manager's *In Search for Excellence*. Kanter has advocated change and innovation in organizations throughout her life, and has developed guidelines for building a change culture in organizations. These guidelines place emphasis on change-focused collaboration at all organizational levels, and on allowing change to occur from the bottom-up.

Contemporary trends

Upon comparing the Post-War and the Industrial eras, one can notice a shift in the focus of organizational development approaches between the two periods. In the Industrial Era, emphasis has consistently been placed on the design of optimal procedures and organizational structures by managers, and their enforcement from the top-down. In contrast, the Post-War Era presents a clear trend toward more participatory management styles and a shift of interest from purely structural to social issues. However, the organizational development ideas in these two eras share one common characteristic. Most of them emerged from academic investigations and hands-on experiences in *manufacturing* settings.

However, the economic environment in most countries has been witnessing rapid changes since the mid-1970s, particularly in the developed and developing nations. In the United States, for example, the number of white-collar workers surpassed that of blue-collar workers at around 1976, which means that work in general has gradually become more knowledge intensive, requiring better educated workers. Estimates by the Organization for Economic Cooperation and Development (OECD) suggest that in the 1990s for every three dollars spent in the United States and several other developed countries, around two dollars are spent on services. A large percentage of service sector sales come from companies that sell some form of data product—e.g. computer software, financial indexes, and news in general. These macroeconomic trends have similarly been observed in individual organizations. Some of our recent studies show that over 70 percent of exchanges within organizations involve information (e.g. memos, faxes, and electronic mail), as opposed to tangible things like parts, raw materials, or tools (Kock and McQueen, 1996; Kock et al., 1997), even when the object of analysis are manufacturing organizations.

It is no wonder, thus, that one of the main organizational development movements in the 1990s, the business process reengineering movement, has from its inception in the early 1990s been heavily focused on service activities. The reengineering movement emerged from the work of two consultants, both with solid academic backgrounds —Michael Hammer (who worked in collaboration with James Champy) and Thomas Davenport (who worked in collaboration with James Short). Unlike some of their organizational development predecessors in the Industrial and Post-War eras, Hammer and Davenport built on the work of practitioners, mostly executives from large corporations, to develop the idea of reengineering. Among other companies, they studied how Ford had dramatically improved its accounts payable process; IBM Credit its financing quotation process; Mutual Benefit Life its new policy issue process. None of these improvements was originally done under the reengineering flag. Nevertheless, due to their underlying similarities, all were later reported as successful cases of business process reengineering.

The term *reengineering* refers to radical organizational redesign projects, particularly when they are focused on cross-departmental *processes* (or sets of interrelated activities). A *process* is like a recipe to bake a cake. It has a set of interrelated activities that must be carried out in a certain order, using certain raw materials and tools, and whose final output is a product that is going to be consumed or used by someone (e.g. a delicious chocolate cake). In an organizational context, a process can be understood as a set of interrelated activities, usually carried out by teams, whose outputs are the goods or services that are typically sold by an organization to its customers (the concept of *process* is discussed in more detail in Chapter 2).

Reengineering emerged as a reaction to the TQM movement, which in turn was largely based on Deming and Juran's ideas. According to Hammer and Champy, TQM projects usually led to only 5 to 15 percent improvements in process productivity, while reengineering could lead to improvements of as much as 300 percent. They also argued that, in spite of TQM's history of success in the US, it was better tailored to the Japanese than to the American culture. According to them, the radical approach taken by reengineering fitted the American ingenuity and creativity much better than the incremental, "small-minded" approach taken by TQM. Moreover, radical process redesign as proposed by reengineering could only happen with the creative use of information technology, which was well in tune with the explosion of the use of networked computers seen in the 1980s and 1990s.

Reengineering went from an idea in the early 1990s to a US$ 50 billion management consulting industry at around 1995. By then, a large number of reported cases of reengineering failure (estimated at around 70 percent of all reengineering attempts) were pushing the movement into a passing fad status. Among the explanations for such a high failure rate was that reengineering had clearly borrowed some of the methods that prevented Taylor's *Scientific Management* from succeeding with well-educated workers. For example, it placed radical process redesign decisions largely in the hands of top managers, key employees and consultants, leaving those who *executed* the processes practically out of the decision loop. The term reengineering was soon linked to corporate downsizing and massive job-cutting, and thus faced strong opposition from workers and their unions.

Analogously to what happened at the end of the Industrial Era, current organizational development approaches are reverting away from reengineering, and leaning towards "softer" approaches that emphasize management-worker collaboration, decentralized access to information and knowledge, and delegation. One such approach is that of *organization learning*, as proposed by MIT professor Peter Senge (Senge, 1990), which focuses on organizational knowledge building and sharing to support optimal teamwork. This approach is essentially a revival of the homonymous approach originally proposed by Argyris, with the basic difference that it takes on a very "soft" and somewhat "evangelical" tone. It appropriately points out the importance of knowledge sharing, but at points adopts a sort of *lets-all-be-friends-and-everything-will-be-great* view of organizations.

Along with a softer orientation, organizational development has seen an increasing interest on knowledge[2] management in the late 1990s. For example, Davenport, who was one of the main figures of the reengineering movement, openly acknowledges reengineering as "something of the past," and has concentrated his efforts on the study and implementation of effective knowledge management techniques in the mid and late 1990s.

A historic view of collaborative computing

As with organizational development, the history of collaborative computing can be split into a few distinct chronological phases. Even though the widespread use of collaborative technologies is closely related to the implementation of local and wide area networks, particularly the Internet, a few precocious projects were developed based on early mainframes.

The history of collaborative computing can be organized around four main phases: (1) the Mainframe Era; (2) the establishment of computer networks; (3) the expansion of local area networks; and (4) the Internet Era. Each of these phases is marked by the dominance of a particular computer technology and related attempts to develop collaborative technologies. The remainder of this section briefly discusses each of these phases individually.

The Mainframe Era

As its name implies, this phase was marked by a dominance of large computer systems, usually known as *mainframes*. It goes from the early 1950s, with the emergence of the first mainframe assembly lines, to the late 1960s, with the first major computer networking projects. A growing presence of computers in organizations and an almost complete lack of concern about collaborative computer support distinguish this phase.

Typical mainframe configurations involve a large central computer (the mainframe) connected to a number of "dumb" terminals—i.e. terminals with very limited or no processing capacity of their own. Unlike the server-client local and wide area network configurations seen today, where client workstations are equipped with powerful processors, mainframe terminals are used only as input-output devices.

In the Mainframe Era, computers were used because of their data processing power, rather than their potential for supporting communication among groups of workers. Nevertheless, such ability was explored around the end of this period as new operating systems with rudimentary (compared with what is available today) synchronous and asynchronous collaborative features were developed[3]. One example of such early collaborative operating systems is Multics, developed at the Massachusetts Institute of Technology and first installed in 1967 on a General Electric GE-635 mainframe.

Although terminals allowed decentralized access to information, this was prevented by a high hourly cost of mainframes. For example, the cost of an IBM-7094 in 1966 was approximately $2 million, while its life span was approximately five years. This means an hourly cost of about $45, at a time when workers earned as little as $1 per hour. Therefore, in an obvious mismatch with the organizational development ideas of this time, information was extremely centralized in the Mainframe Era. All data storage and processing activities were performed by employees of *central data processing departments*, which meant that requests for vital information to perform organizational activities (such as customer contact information) had to necessarily be sent to and fulfilled by these departments. This situation persisted for many years, and was dramatically changed with the advent and expansion of the local area networks. This occurred only after the first computer networks (usually large and geographically distributed ones) were set in place, mostly through government-funded projects in the US.

The establishment of computer networks

This phase ranges from the late 1960s to mid-1980s. It began with a major development in 1967 (official start date according to most accounts), the ARPANET project, which provided the basis on which the now ubiquitous Internet has evolved.

The ARPANET project was began under the auspices of the Advanced Research Projects Agency (ARPA), a branch of the US Department of Defense (DOD). Its main goal was to build a network of shared computational resources by interconnecting major universities and research centers in the US.

A major limitation of early mainframes and their operating systems was their lack of interoperability. In 1966, mainframes of a certain brand could only exchange data with other mainframes of the same brand. IBM mainframes could interact only with other IBM mainframes; Burroughs interacted only with Burroughs; General Electric with General Electric; and so on. One of the ARPANET project's main goals was to put together a heterogeneous network connecting IBMs, GEs, and all other mainframe brands together. Another goal was to build a network of dispersed and powerful computer resources so that, in the event of a war-related attack from the Soviet Union[4], only part of the United States' computing power would be actually affected.

At the same time as the ARPANET project began, smaller mainframes were developed; some of which with processing power similar to earlier mainframes. This was enabled by the development of *integrated circuits*, which combined many transistors into a single dedicated *chip*. Such small mainframes were dubbed *minicomputers*. As integrated circuits became smaller and smaller, and the number of transistors they combined into a chip increased, minicomputers later evolved into *microcomputers* with ever-expanding processing power and storage capacity.

One of ARPANET's component systems was an early and rudimentary version of electronic mail. Given little importance in the beginning, electronic mail rapidly became one of the most widely used components of the ARPANET (Sproull and Kiesler, 1991). By 1971, there were about 37 hosts connected to the ARPANET network, each serving many dumb terminals. Virtually all users of these terminals could now communicate with each other through electronic mail, and so they did. Researchers, university professors, and students began using the system for both formal and information communication. Physically dispersed research groups emerged, pushing ARPANET into extending beyond the United States to England and Norway in 1973. The seed of the modern collaborative technologies had been planted.

At the same time, pioneering implementations of systems to support collaborative work occurred elsewhere, mostly using asynchronous technologies and in very experimental ways. These early implementations led to the first organized workshop on *computer-supported cooperative work* (CSCW), a term that was later replaced with others such as groupware, computer-support collaboration, and collaborative computing (Grudin, 1994a). This workshop was conducted in 1984, and was followed two years later by the first international conference on CSCW in Austin, Texas (Bannon, 1993).

The expansion of local area networks

This phase goes from the mid-1980s to the early 1990s, and owes much of its existence to the development and widespread use of personal computers. With the development in the mid 1970s of large-scale integrated circuits, whose transistor capacity was much higher than the normal integrated circuits, computers became smaller in size and more powerful. As a result, the first personal computers, or PCs, were developed. PCs (also referred to as microcomputers, or micros) were usually much cheaper than their predecessors, the minicomputers. The first of all PCs is believed to have been Altair, a $400 computer for which Microsoft's founders Bill Gates and Paul Allen developed a simple BASIC interpreter. At that time, Allen was a college dropout working for Honeywell, and Gates a freshman at Harvard. BASIC, which stands for Beginner's All-Purpose Symbolic Instruction Code, was one of the first popular computer programming languages.

The development of Altair was followed by the release of increasingly more sophisticated PCs, which relied on new central processing unit (CPU) technologies developed by Intel, Motorola and other CPU manufacturers. In 1978, Intel released its 8086 processor, which contained over 29,000 transistors. The Intel 8088, released in 1979, was used by International Business Machines (IBM) in their famous and much cloned IBM PC.

As microcomputers grew cheaper and more powerful, established software developers started shifting their efforts toward popular PC platforms. Myriad new software developers entered the PC application development market, taking advantage of lower entry barriers. With the development of micro-mainframe connection cards, such as the once widely used IRMA cards, PCs could be used both as independent computers and dumb terminals. Due to their newly obtained dual functionally, PCs became an attractive alternative to dumb terminals used with mainframes. This paved the path for the *downsizing*[5] of applications from mainframes to local area PC networks, whenever possible. Applications that required light processing power, low storage capacity, or that could benefit from distributed processing arrangements, became the object of massive downsizing.

Once-very-wealthy companies that relied heavily on mainframe sales for financial grow saw their market shrink and revenues dwindle. At the same time, PC and local area network companies experienced a tremendous growth. As the PC manufacturing industry became more competitive and PC prices plummeted, the importance of software that linked several PCs and resources (e.g. printers, fax machines) increased. The market for such software systems, called *local area network operating systems*, skyrocketed. Many companies tried to enter this market, but its undisputed leader in the 1980s was Novell Corporation, a Utah-based company that launched its first local area network operating system in 1983.

Local area networks (LANs) emerged as a standard tool for organizational development in firms of all sizes. At the beginning, one of the main advantages of having a LAN connecting several PCs and computer peripherals was that it enabled the sharing of what were then relatively expensive resources, such as printers and large-capacity hard disks. In time, however, LANs also progressed as a mechanism to implement and consolidate some of the organizational development approaches that became popular in the 1980s. At this time the total quality management and the excellence movements called for, among other things, worker empowerment through delegation and decentralized information access, for which LANs were seen by many as the ideal support tool.

Many synchronous and asynchronous collaborative technologies were developed in this phase. Some of them, such as Information Lenz and the Coordinator, extended the common set of features exhibited by early electronic mail systems.

Others, such as GroupSystems, Teamfocus, and MeetingWorks, provided support for decision-oriented face-to-face meetings. Still others, such as Lotus Notes and Domino, operated as suites on which customized collaborative technologies could be developed to support specific group processes. Most of these technologies result from the work of researchers in universities and government as well as corporate research centers. The following phase, the Internet Era, has seen many of these applications migrate from LAN to Internet-based platforms.

The Internet Era

The Internet Era began in the early 1990s and extends to the present day. Its emergence is largely due to LANs' limitations regarding remote communication and data access. Similarly to isolated PCs, isolated LANs need special devices and communication media to share data over long distances. While LANs can link PCs in the same building or campus, without wide area networks such as ARPANET, PCs in different LANs are unable to communicate. Links between LANs should be built for this to happen.

The service sector growth seen in this period, and particularly the growth in information industries (e.g. software development, TV news, newspapers, financial information firms), contributed to a huge increase in the amount of data that had to be handled by organizations on a daily basis. Besides, this period was marked by a fast pace of change, which called for radical change approaches to organizational development such as business process reengineering. Such fast pace of change also required that the data sitting in isolated LANs be moved around faster than ever before, especially in the increasing number of companies spanning city, state and even national boundaries.

One of the first successful attempts to link computers separated by large distances was the already mentioned ARPANET project. However, the main goal of this project was to link mainframe computers, not PCs already connected in LANs. In time, basic devices (which included their own hardware and software, and sometimes ran on PCs) called *bridges* were developed, to link two or more remotely located LANs. A *bridge* can use different media to connect two or more LANs. Many of the early *bridges* used private telephone lines (copper wires) with speeds of only up to 64 kilobits per second for inter-LAN connectivity (i.e. a single one-megabyte file would take over 2 minutes to be transferred between LANs). These speeds increased as new data compression techniques, thicker copper wires, and new communication media (e.g. fiber optics) became commercially available.

However, connecting LANs through *bridges* was expensive and complex, particularly when several LANs had to be interconnected. If users connected to a LAN at one company wanted to access data located in another LAN at a different company, then at least one dedicated *bridge* between these two LANs would have to be set up and administered. What was really needed was something simpler and less expensive than that. Perhaps a single public infrastructure that allowed multiple LANs to be linked, regardless of the existing hardware and operating system configurations. With this in mind, Tim Berners-Lee proposed, in 1989, a global hypertext project, to be later known as the World Wide Web (also known as WWW or the *web*). This work was started in October 1990, and led to the development of the first web server and browser, and early specifications of the HTTP communication protocol, and the HTML language.

Contrary to a popular perception, the web is not the Internet. The web is an abstract collection of web "sites" that uses the physical infrastructure provided by the Internet. The Internet, in turn, evolved from the initial infrastructure set in place for the ARPANET project. In 1987, its administration was taken over from the US Department of Defense by the National Science Foundation. The Internet was not very popular by then, or in the years immediately following Berners-Lee's project. It really started to show signs of exponential growth in 1993, when the popular web browser Mosaic was developed at the University of Illinois, Urbana-Champaign. In mid-1993, the web had just a few hundred web hosts[6]; in 1994 it reached about one million; over four million in 1995; over eight million in 1996; and over 20 million in 1997. Popular commercial web browsers succeed Mosaic, notably Netscape Navigator (developed by members of the original Mosaic's team) and Microsoft's Internet Explorer. Such browsers are today used by hundreds of millions of users around the world to obtain information, purchase goods and services, and build personal relationships over the Internet.

The advent of the Internet Era led collaboration technologies to move from the LAN environment to the Internet, mostly as client-server systems running on platforms made of generic, platform-independent web browsers (on the client side), and platform-dependent web servers (on the server side). Interfaces to popular electronic mail packages such as Groupwise (by Novell Corporation) were developed so users could access their mailboxes using any standard web browser. In the mid-1990s, such companies as Qualcomm and Microsoft offered free web-based electronic mail, available to anyone with access to, again, a standard web browser. Synchronous "chat" tools were developed to run on web pages, which allow for simultaneous two-way transfer of voice and text, threatening to bite into the profitable long-distance telephone market. Video and audio streaming allowed for real-time video and audio transfer and broadcasting, even through narrow bandwidth media such as copper wires.

The web browser interface has become, in the Internet Era, the standard for computer-mediated collaboration. The low-cost public infrastructure provided by the Internet brought about seamless integration of data and resources to what was formerly a chaotic mix of dispersed LANs, most of them isolated from the other LANs. In the Internet Era, the problem is no longer accessing information located elsewhere, but to cope with information overload.

Summary and concluding remarks

From a historic perspective, organizational development has progressed hand-in-hand with new management ideas. At the same time, the success of computer technologies in general, and collaborative technologies in particular, have depended in part on the adequacy with which they were able to support popular organizational development ideas of the time. This explains, to some extent, the proliferation of collaborative "knowledge management" computer tools in the late 1990s, which occurs at a time when there is heightened interest in organizational development approaches that promote cross-functional knowledge sharing.

The evolution of organizational development can be split into three main phases

—the Industrial Era, the Post-War Era, and the current phase. The Industrial Era was marked by an emphasis on the design of optimal procedures and organizational structures by managers, and their enforcement down the organizational ladder.

In the Post-War Era the emphasis shifted from purely structural to social issues, and top-down control was replaced with participatory management. While being essentially different, the Industrial and Post-War eras were primarily concerned with manufacturing activities and organizations. This started to change in the late 1980s, with the advent of organizational development ideas targeted at the service sector, where most knowledge intensive industries are now located.

Analogously to the organizational development evolution, a historical look at the evolution of collaborative technologies can be divided into four main phases— the Mainframe Era, the establishment of computer networks, the expansion of local area networks, and the Internet Era.

In the Mainframe Era, which was marked by the hegemony of large mainframe computers, collaborative technologies were practically nonexistent. In this phase, which went from the early 1950s to approximately 1965, collaborative technologies were confined to rudimentary collaboration tools built in mainframe operating systems.

The phase where the establishment of computer networks occurred ranged from the late 1960s to mid-1980s. This phase was marked by the development of the ARPANET project, which began in 1967 under the auspices of the Advanced Research Projects Agency (ARPA), a branch of the US Department of Defense (DOD). The main goal of the ARPANET project was to build a network of shared computational resources by interconnecting major universities and research centers in the US. A few initially neglected component systems of the ARPANET network, particularly its simple electronic mail tool, planted the seed for the future development of more sophisticated collaborative technologies.

From the mid-1980s to the early 1990s, the organizational world has seen the expansion of the local area networks, which connected personal computers. This phase owes much of its existence to the development and widespread use of powerful and reasonably cheap microcomputers (a.k.a. personal computers), as was the most prolific in terms of the development of new collaborative technologies.

Most of the collaborative technologies made available in the phase that followed the expansion of local area networks, the Internet Era, are based on technologies developed in the preceding phase. The Internet Era extends from the early 1990s to the present day. Its emergence is largely due to remote communication and data access limitations of local area networks, which supported the interconnection of microcomputers located relatively near each other (e.g. in the same building or campus). The advent of the Internet Era led collaboration technologies to move from the local area network environment to the Internet, mostly as client-server systems running on platforms made of generic, platform-independent web browsers (on the client side), and platform-dependent web servers (on the server side).

In the Internet Era, the web browser interface has become the standard for computer-mediated collaboration. The low-cost public infrastructure provided by the Internet brought about seamless integration of data and resources to what was formerly a chaotic mix of separate local area networks. In the Internet Era, the problem of accessing remotely located information has been solved. The real challenge in this phase is to deal with the explosion of information available at our fingertips.

Endnotes

[1] More recently, such top corporate control companies have often been referred to as *holding* companies.

[2] The concepts of data, information and knowledge are defined and contrasted in Chapter 3.

[3] *Synchronous* group collaboration requires same-time communication (e.g. a teleconference), whereas *asynchronous* collaboration usually involves time-disconnected communication (e.g. the use of electronic-mail for work-related communication).

[4] The Cold War between the US and former ally, Soviet Union, was well under way by this time.

[5] The term *downsizing* has different meanings, depending on the context where it is used. Popular business magazines often use it to refer to the reduction in the size of organizations, often caused by massive layoffs and division sellouts. In information systems circles, the term is used to refer to the migration of computer applications from mainframes to local area networks.

[6] Web hosts store *web sites*, which in turn store text, video, audio and pictures that can be downloaded by web browsers (e.g. Mosaic, Netscape Navigator, and Internet Explorer).

Chapter 2

What is a Process?

The pervasiveness of process improvement

Process improvement can be defined as the analysis and redesign of organizational processes to achieve performance and competitiveness gains. The idea that process-focused improvement can be used as a tool to boost organizational performance and competitiveness is not new. In fact, process improvement has been the basis of several widely adopted management approaches such as total quality management, business process reengineering, and organizational learning. As the following sections briefly show, process-focused improvement can be seen as a unifying concept of these management approaches.

Total quality management

One of the main tenets of the total quality management movement is that the focus of improvement should be on *processes* rather than *problems*. Moreover, when one carefully looks at the causes of organizational problems (e.g. high costs, low quality, deficient worker productivity), it becomes clear that over 80 percent of them are process-related, whereas only 20 percent or less are to be blamed on the people who carry out process activities (Deming, 1986).

This new perspective constituted a shift from the old view that problems in organizations are caused by workers' negligence and their disregard of/for management-set rules for process execution. Organizational norms of accepted behavior, formal job definitions, rigidly set communication channels, hierarchical structures, inflexible computer systems, as well as reward systems are just a few elements of organizational process design. It is in these elements, argued the total quality management movement, that most improvement opportunities are to be found.

Business process reengineering

Unlike the total quality management movement, which seems to have been built around a common set of concepts and propositions, the business process reengineering movement has been characterized by the existence of different schools of thought. From the beginning, at least two schools of thought could be identified.

Computer expert and management consultant Michael Hammer led the radical and more "popular" school. It proposed reengineering as a totally new and revolutionary approach for process improvement, and argued for a complete departure from the incremental process improvement approach which characterized total quality management (Hammer, 1990; Hammer and Champy, 1993).

The other school, more "conservative" in its expectations, was led by University of Texas' professor Thomas Davenport. It proposed radical core process redesign as just a new tool for process improvement (Davenport and Short, 1990; Davenport, 1993), and argued for the combined use of this new process improvement tool with others, such as total quality management itself (Davenport, 1993a).

The radical reengineering school was initially much more popular than the conservative school, which is exemplified by the fact that Hammer and Champy's (1993) book *Reengineering the Corporation* sold over two million copies by 1995. Davenport's (1993) book *Process Innovation* sold less than 100,000 copies in the same period (a sizeable figure yet only a small fraction of Hammer and Champy's book sales).

However, two years after the publication of Hammer and Champy's (1993) book, the radical school was split. Due to a high rate of failure in reengineering projects (often reported as 70 to 75 percent), the radical tone of this school was slightly softened in Hammer and Stanton's (1995) sequel *The Reengineering Revolution*, though its authors persistently clung to the idea that reengineering was a "revolutionary" approach.

At the same time, a new and short-lived reengineering branch was begun by one of its forerunners, CSC Index's head James Champy, focusing on shifting *management* paradigms, as opposed to "simply" redesigning *processes* (Champy, 1995). Champy argued that the high rate of failure in reengineering projects was to a large extent caused by the fact that while processes were being radically redesigned, the way managers viewed their organizations was not. According to Champy, this dichotomy had led to a widespread lack of management support for reengineering attempts, which was indeed found to be one of the top reasons why reengineering projects have been reported to fail according to a study by Caldwell (1994). Nevertheless, the arguments put forth by Champy to make his point have been found to be less than convincing and somewhat "evangelical" (Wensley, 1996), and the impact of his 1995 book was small among the torrent of reengineering books and articles published in the same year.

Both the radical and the more conservative schools led by Hammer and Davenport recently converged on one main point —that the main contribution of the business process reengineering movement was not to propose a radical and revolutionary approach for organizational change. Its main contribution has been increased management awareness about the importance of *processes* and the advantages of a *process* focus in organizational design and improvement (Davenport et al., 1996; Hammer, 1996).

Organizational learning

Process improvement also seems at the core of what is often referred to as the *learning organization* movement. MIT professor and author of the seminal book *The Fifth Discipline* (Senge, 1990) Peter Senge is believed by many to be the "father" of the learning organizations movement. However, Senge's work builds largely on ideas developed a decade earlier by University of Lancaster professor Peter Checkland, in the general field of system dynamics (Checkland, 1981; Checkland and Scholes, 1990), and by Harvard professor Chris Argyris.

One particularly important contribution by Argyris has been the concept of *double-loop learning*, which he contrasts with that of *single-loop learning* (Argyris, 1977; 1992). Argyris seems to often adopt a cybernetic perspective (i.e. a control-centered perspective) in his interpretation of learning, hence his choice of explaining the concepts of single and double-loop learning by often using analogies with control devices— e.g. a thermostat-activated heater (Argyris, 1977, p. 116).

A device that senses a decrease in the temperature of a room and changes the amount of heat that it gives off, in order to maintain the room's temperature constant, engages in what Argyris refers to as single-loop learning. This is a "reactive" behavior that involves little knowledge and that therefore can easily be automated. It does not involve the understanding of the mechanics of heat transfer and fluid dynamics.

Double-loop learning, on the other hand, would be the type of learning involved in understanding the process through which variations of the room's temperature occur, and devising a more efficient approach to maintain the room's temperature constant. Single-loop learning alone would never lead to the identification of an air leak close to one of the windows, for example. It would therefore lead to a situation in which the room's temperature would be kept constant at a higher cost than it could have been otherwise (assuming that the higher electricity bill would be more expensive than fixing the leak).

In the example above, the identification of the leak could only result from an analysis of the heat transfer *process* in the room. The understanding of the mechanics of air heating and flow in different points of the room would eventually reveal that there was a disproportionate amount of heat being transferred near the window. This is one example of the similarity between what is called learning, in the organizational learning movement, and process-focused improvement. I will extend this discussion later in Chapter 4 (Process improvement and organizational learning), but now I should try to answer the question with which I started this chapter: What is a process?

What is a process? Different views

As a concept becomes more abstract, so does the discrepancy in the ways different people construe the concept. A concept that refers to a tangible object, like that of a *chair* for example, is likely to be understood more or less in the same way by two or more people. If one person says "...*then I sat on this big, soft, blue chair...*", the other will probably be able to visualize the scene in more or less the same way as the first person did.

With abstract concepts such as that of a *process*, however, this shared mental visualization is much less likely to be achieved without further clarification. One of the reasons for this difficulty is that abstractions are not perceived by our five senses as "real" objects like a chair is (e.g. we can see and touch a chair), and therefore must be understood based on abstract models. If these models do not exist, or are too rough and incomplete, then a sense of perplexity often takes on. This phenomenon is an instance of what has been called "dissociation of sentience and knowledge," which has been discussed in length by Harvard professor Shoshana Zuboff in her book *In the Age of the Smart Machine* (Zuboff, 1988; 1996).

The dissociation between sensorial stimuli and understanding has been associated with adaptation problems faced by workers that are taken away from the shop floor, where they have direct and often physical contact with the machines they operate, and into computer-operated control rooms. In the control rooms, workers must understand the machines they control as points in a production process (which is itself an abstract entity). This may not be easy for factory workers, as suggested the following quote from one of Zuboff's interviewees (Zuboff, 1996, p. 197):

> It is very different now...It is hard to get used to not being out there with the process. I miss it a lot. I miss being able to see it. You can see when the pulp runs over a vat. You know what's happening.

Processes, as most abstract entities, need to be modeled in some way to be understood. And, more importantly, two or more people must understand the processes in roughly the same way. Models, however, irrespective of how complex they are, are in most of the cases limited representations of whatever they are supposed to represent, whether these are real objects or abstract entities. A given representation of a transistor, for example, can help one predict how it will be "fired" (i.e. amplify an electrical input) when an electrical impulse of a certain voltage is applied to it. However, the same representation can be almost useless to predict the operation of the same transistor when its input is an alternate current whose frequency is above a certain level (e.g. in discreet analog telecommunication circuits). Similarly, a given representation of a car such as an owner's manual diagram explaining the basic operation of the car, can be detailed enough for someone who wants to *drive* the car and yet useless to someone who needs to *repair* the car. In fact, perhaps the only characteristic that is shared by all models is that they are all incomplete representations.

A few main types of process models, or *views*, are discussed in the following sub-sections. These views lead, as discussed above, to *incomplete* representations of processes, and therefore should be understood in terms of their pros and cons in today's information and knowledge-intensive organizational environments. I try to contribute to this understanding in my discussion of each of the views.

The workflow view

Although there seems to be little agreement on what a process is or the main elements that make it up are, the predominant view among academics and practitioners seems to be that of a *set of interrelated activities* (Hunt, 1996; Ould, 1995). In this sense, processes are seen as activity flows (a.k.a. *workflows*) composed of activities that bear some sort of relationship with each other (White and Fischer,

1994). This means that, if activities are not perceived as interrelated, then they are not part of the same process.

While this is an interesting conceptualization of processes, there is a catch. Processes are not real structures. That is, sets of interrelated activities are just *mental abstractions* that allow us to understand organizations and how they operate. Therefore, processes are what we *perceive* them to be— i.e. what our mental models tell us about them. If a manager perceives the activities *(a) design a new product* and *(b) market a new product* as being closely related, then the manager will draw a workflow model of the process *launch a new product* as being made up of activities in both the product design and marketing departments. Such model will be one of a cross-departmental process. However, if the manager sees those activities as separate and independent, then his (her) view of the process will either be incomplete, or emphasize the role of one of the two departments (Vennix, 1996, p. 15).

The difficulty discussed above is a direct result of the fact that processes are mental abstractions (together with our mental representations of everything else in the world), and of the worst type—they are mental abstractions of abstract entities, since *processes* are not "real", tangible things. That is, unlike tangible things such as a chair or a desk, processes are intangible. They cannot be seen or touched. This characteristic will affect most of what I will say in this book about process improvement and organizational learning.

The terms "interrelated activities" and *workflow* can be understood differently by different people in the field of process management. This can be an obstacle to

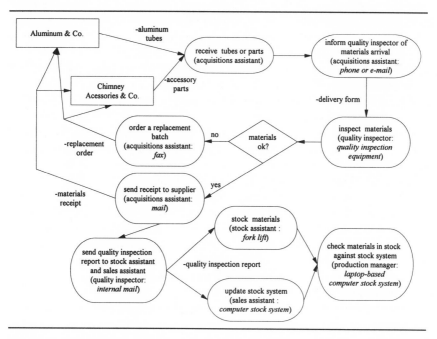

Figure 2.1: "Receive materials" process of a chimney manufacturer Adapted from Kock et al. (1997, p. 72)

achieving a basic goal of any workflow representation, which is the identification of the types of relationships between activities. In fact, such identification of types of relationships has not been a widespread concern, with a few exceptions —see e.g. Malone and Crowston's (1994) discussion about workflow coordination, and Schmidt's (1994) conceptualization of processes involving coordination of different functions. I believe that a categorization of basic activity relationships in processes can be helpful in identifying organizational processes from a workflow perspective.

Our study and consulting experience suggests that there are at least three main types of relationships between activities in processes, which are referred to as: (a) *common predecessor*, (b) *common successor*, and (c) *predecessor-successor*. These relationships are illustrated in the "receive materials" process of a chimney manu- facturer shown in Figure 2.1, where activities are shown within oval shapes and the arrows indicate the flow of execution of the activities in the process.

A rectangular shape represents an external supplier of the process, whereas a diamond shape indicates a decision point in the process. Each activity is described by its name, followed (within parentheses) by the organizational function that carries out the activity and the italicized name of the main tool used by this function. Freestanding text beginning with a "dash" is used to describe a "product" (which can be a piece of data or a material thing) that flows between activities.

The *common predecessor* relationship joins together activities that have a common immediate predecessor activity. In the process shown in Figure 2.1, the activities *order a replacement batch*, carried out by the acquisitions assistant usually by fax, and *send a receipt to supplier*, also carried out by the acquisitions assistant typically using ordinary mail, display this type of relationship. Both activities have the same immediate predecessor, the activity *inspect materials*, done by the quality inspector using specialized quality inspection equipment. This common predecessor must be carried out before each of these two interrelated activities.

The *common successor* relationship connects activities that have a common immediate successor activity. The activities *stock materials* and *update stock system*, the former done by the stock assistant with the use of a forklift and the latter by the sales assistant on a computerized stock system, are connected through a *common successor* relationship. Both activities have a common successor, the activity *check materials in stock against stock system*, done by the production manager by walking through the stock warehouse and comparing it with the inventory database using a laptop-based version of a computerized stock system.

The *predecessor-successor* relationship, the most common type of relationship between activities, joins up two activities that take place in sequence, one after the other. Note that, as with the two types of relationships describe above, a *predecessor- successor* relationship can exist even if no materials or data flow between activities. The activities *receive tubes or parts* and *inform quality inspector of materials arrival* are connected by a *predecessor-successor* relationship as they can only be carried out in sequence, the second after the first.

The process of creating workflow representations of processes, typically called flowcharting, is, according to Harrington (1991, p. 86): "... an invaluable tool for understanding the inner workings of, and relationships between, business pro- cesses." Irrespective of this opinion, however, one important point must be made about workflow representations of processes, such as the flowchart in Figure 2.1.

Although flowcharts can show the data or materials that flow between activities in a process, these data or materials *do not actually flow* between activities. Hence, the data flow representation in flowcharts can be somewhat misleading. For example, the delivery form that apparently flows between the activities *inform quality inspector of materials arrival* and *inspect materials*, in reality flows between the organizational functions that carry out these activities— acquisitions assistant and quality inspector. The delivery form is a data repository that allows for the exchange of information between these two functions. This shortcoming of the workflow view can be of significant importance if the focus of a process redesign attempt is the data flow, not the activity configuration in a process. This is because the workflow view "hides" information about how data flow in organizational processes (Kock and McQueen, 1996). And, as it is discussed in Chapter 3 (Data, information and knowledge), a focus on data flows is in general advisable, since the flow of data is increasingly becoming a central concern in projects targeted at boosting organizational competitiveness.

There are a number of variations of workflow representations similar to the one shown in Figure 2.1. The workflow in Figure 2.1 itself is an adaptation of the ANSI standard flow chart, and has been extensively used in our work with process improvement groups—see Kock (1995) or Appendix A for a description of the use of this flowcharting tool in process improvement groups. Flowchart variations are the block diagram, functional flowchart, functional time-line flowchart, and geographic flowchart—see, for example, Harrington (1991) for a more detailed discussion of these.

The data flow view

Another traditional view of business processes is the data flow view, where processes are seen as data processing entities. Data flow representations have been largely used in the 1980s by systems analysts as an important component of what are known as *structured* systems analysis and design techniques (Davis, 1983)—a predecessor of the now ubiquitous *object-oriented* analysis and design approach (Somerville, 1992).

Data flow representations have been used chiefly to understand the flow of data within processes and later automate this flow "as is", rather than to redesign (that is, change) processes. This "automation-of-old-processes" approach has been the target of strong criticism in the early 1990s, often being described as the main cause of the low return on investment in information technology observed in both the 1970s and 1980s. According to Hackett (1990), the service sector has been particularly affected by this low return on investment in information technology. Such return has steadily declined to even negative figures (that is, the investment in IT has led to a *decrease* in productivity) in a number of service industries such as banking and insurance.

Like the workflow view of processes, the data flow view can be expressed through a family of graphical representations, from which the most widely used is the *data flow diagram*, or simply DFD (Gore and Stubbe, 1988; Pressman, 1987). An example of DFD obtained from the analysis of the flow of data between the restaurants and the central kitchen of an Italian restaurant chain is shown in Figure

2.2. A rectangular shape represents a data source or destination—the restaurant manager and the central kitchen manager functions, in the figure. Arrows indicate the flow of data, which are described by freestanding text located beside the arrows. Oval shapes represent activities. Open-ended rectangles represent data repositories.

The process mapped through the DFD in Figure 2.2 starts with the manager of one of the restaurants of the chain contacting the manager of a central kitchen, where all dish items are prepared. The restaurant manager tells the manager of the central kitchen that the restaurant is short of some specific items (e.g. Bolognese sauce, spaghetti, Italian bread). The manager of the central kitchen then fills out a form in which he specifies some out-of-stock items and the restaurant that needs them, and hands this form into the assistant manager's inbox. Approximately every two hours, the assistant manager (of the central kitchen) goes through the forms in his inbox and generates and stores in his outbox the orders to be produced by the cooking team. He tries to optimize the work of the cooking team when doing this scheduling, by grouping requests that require the same resources (e.g. ingredients, cooking equipment). The cooking team then collects the orders from the assistant manager's outbox and prepares the Italian dish items ordered on a first-come-first-serve basis, packing and stocking them in the delivery room as soon as they are ready. Delivery forms are filled out and attached to each of the packed items for the restaurants, which are periodically delivered by the central kitchen's delivery team.

Although an incomplete model of real processes, representations based on the data flow view of processes such as DFDs show in a relatively clear way how data flow and are stored in processes. As such, one can reasonably expect these representations to be more appropriate than workflow-based representations, such as flowcharts, in some cases. This is true especially in the analysis of processes where the flow of data is particularly intense.

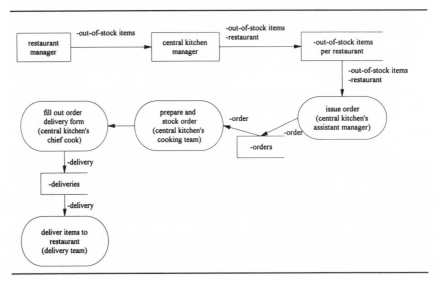

Figure 2.2: "Fulfill order" process of a central kitchen at an Italian restaurant chain Adapted from Kock (1995a, p. 44)

A dramatic increase in data flow has been predicted as one of the characteristics of today's and the near future's economy, particularly in developed countries (Drucker, 1989; Toffler, 1970; 1991). Hence, it is reasonable to expect that representations based on the data flow view of processes are more likely to be useful in process improvement attempts than representations based on the workflow view. As mentioned before in this chapter, the latter type of representations tend to provide a poorer picture of how data flows, preventing the identification of, for example, data "buffers". Data buffers are organizational functions (rectangular shapes in DFDs) whose job in a given process is to transfer data between other organizational functions. These "buffers" are therefore strong candidates to be removed from the process and be replaced by information technology applications. This is the case in Figure 2.2 of the function *central kitchen manager*, who acts as a buffer between the restaurant manager and the assistant manager of the central kitchen. In the process analyzed, the manager of the central kitchen receives data from the restaurant manager and stores it into a data repository that will be used as input by the assistant manager of the central kitchen to generate an order. A more efficient version of the process would have the restaurant manager storing this data herself, with no mediation of the manager of the central kitchen, who could use his time to do other things.

When mapping processes through either flowcharts or DFDs one may wonder how much detail to show in the diagram. After all, the activities in a process representation can also be seen as sub-processes themselves, which can, in turn, be broken into new activities. In fact, seeing the activities of processes as lower-level processes and generating more detailed diagrams by "exploding" these lower-level processes is a common practice in both flowcharting and DFD generation (Davis, 1983; Maull et al., 1995; Pressman, 1987). In doing so, however, two simple guidelines are suggested (Kock and McQueen, 1996):

- Each graphical representation of a process should not have more than 15 symbols.
- In a process improvement context, the level of detail one should search for when modeling processes should be defined by the *breadth* of improvement sought.

The first guideline is based on studies about general human cognitive limitations relating graphical representations and diagrams used in systems analysis and design (Kock, 1995a).

The second guideline is based on a relatively new concept —that of *breath* of process improvement (Hall et al., 1993). Roughly speaking, the breadth of improvement correlates the number of departments affected by process improvement decisions. The larger the breath of improvement, the less process detail is necessary. If one wishes to improve processes that cut across several (perhaps all) of the departments of an organization, the process representation should comprise little detail about sub-processes that belong to individual departments. As a general rule of thumb, the total number of high-level processes used to effectively represent any organizational unit can be anywhere between 10 and 20 (Hammer and Champy, 1993; Maull et al., 1995).

Other process views

Although the two process views discussed above—the workflow and the data flow view—are in my opinion the most relevant ones for this book, there are other views of processes. Among these are the systems view and the object-oriented view, briefly discussed below.

The systems view

The systems view of processes is based on the traditional concept of *system*—an assembly of parts that cannot be understood only as a function of its components. A system can be defined by its *emergent properties*, which are *system* properties and therefore meaningless in terms of the parts that make up the system. This concept is illustrated by Checkland and Scholes (1990, p. 19):

> The vehicular potential of a bicycle is an emergent property of the combined parts of a bicycle when they are assembled in a particular way to make the structured whole.

According to the systems view, a process can be operationally defined as an abstract entity that represents the transformation of inputs into outputs (Childe et al., 1994; Childe, 1995; Kock, 1995a). The process suppliers provide inputs. Outputs are consumed by the process customers. The transformation of inputs into outputs is aimed at adding value to the customers of the process. The inputs and outputs of a process may be of three different types— goods, services, and data (Juran, 1989; Kock and Tomelin, 1996).

While philosophically appealing, the main problem with the systems view of processes is that it adds little to our understanding of the inner workings of a process, and therefore may be of little use to those who try to change the process. According to the systems view, processes are defined by means of sets of emergent properties that characterize them; the relationship between their components being of secondary importance.

In spite of its limitations, the systems view has proved to be more useful than the workflow view in the analysis of very complex (and often "messy") processes such as those related to strategic decision making, for example. These processes typically *cannot* be analyzed as workflows because, among other things, the number of activities and decision points required to represent them is too large to allow for effective modeling. My own experience supports this assumption. In 1992, for example, I tried to analyze one such process in an advertising company, and ended up with a very complicated model made up of more than 150 activities. One could argue that, in this case, taking a systems approach to modeling would have allowed for a better understanding of the process. However, given time and financial constraints that are not often mentioned in textbooks, the firm's management and I simply decided to skip the strategic management process in question and move on to other more analyzable processes.

The object-oriented view

One of the main proponents of the object-oriented view of processes is Ivar

Jacobson, who developed a methodology to model processes as data objects. Jacobson's methodology was based on the concept of *software object* (Jacobson et al., 1995). A software object is a data repository with a number of operations associated to it. These operations are also called *methods* in the technical jargon of object-oriented analysis and programming (Thomas, 1989). A software object typically stores data in its attributes, which are analogous to the attributes of real objects like a chair—e.g. attributes of an object *chair* would be its *color, weight* and *number of legs* (Partridge, 1994).

The object-oriented view can be seen as an extension of the data flow view in which data repositories, represented in DFDs by open-ended rectangles (see Figure 2.2), are permanently linked to activities that change the content of those repositories. There is a clear advantage in adopting this view. Many believe that object-oriented programming is increasingly becoming the dominant software development paradigm (e.g. it has been adopted by most of the major players in the software development industry in the 1990s). Also, the object-oriented view of processes allows for an inexpensive transition between: (a) process analysis and redesign, and (b) the development of new computer systems to support the implementation of the new redesigned processes.

However, the object-oriented view has been criticized by its excessively technical orientation, preventing less sophisticated users (i.e. those who are unfamiliar with object-oriented concepts) from effectively understanding it in its full complexity and adopting it in process improvement projects. Process analysis and design methodologies using object-oriented representations, such as the Unified Modeling Language (UML), are still too complex to be widely accepted and used in organizations, in spite of the fact that UML has been endorsed by heavyweights of the computer community (Meyer, 1998). This has been compounded by the fact that among less sophisticated users are often senior managers who are usually absorbed into strategic management issues and therefore don't have the time to become technically sophisticated. The problem with this situation is that the support of such managers is a fundamental ingredient in successful process improvement initiatives (Davenport, 1993).

Moreover, some recent developments in the software industry have turned the building of computer systems "in-house", which is facilitated by the adoption of the object-oriented view of processes, into an often undesirable and expensive alternative. Buying off-the-shelf applications, quickly prototyping new computer applications, and outsourcing the development of computer systems to enable new organizational processes are seen by many as more desirable approaches made possible by such developments. Among these developments are:

- The emergence of computer-aided software engineering (CASE) tools, which support rapid application development (Martin, 1991);
- The increasing number of powerful and user-friendly general-purpose systems that can rapidly be adapted to perform a diverse range of tasks. For instance, spreadsheets can be used to build flexible small-scale customer databases and cash flow control systems, which previously would have to be developed through traditional computer programming; and

- The proliferation of specialized software development companies in almost all industries, whose software development costs are usually much lower than those of in-house development.

Summary and concluding remarks

The *process* concept has become, in the 1990s, the focus of growing attention from managers, business consultants, and management researchers. This was particularly due to the business process reengineering movement, which apparently fell short of initial expectations yet deeply influenced contemporary management thinking.

In reality, reengineering is nothing but a genre of process improvement. Diverse process improvement approaches may employ entirely different guidelines and analytical tools. Yet, all such approaches share a common focus on organizational processes.

A careful analysis of the history of organizational development shows that process improvement has been an underlying force in many management movements, including the total quality management, business process reengineering, and the organizational learning movements.

The central element of process improvement is the process, and thus it is important that we clearly define this concept. The most widely accepted definition of a process is *a set of interrelated activities*. However precise this definition may sound, it is broad enough to spur different interpretations or "views". The two predominant process views are the *workflow* and *data flow* views.

The workflow view focuses on the understanding of processes as groups of interrelated activities, among which data or material products are exchanged. Although a very intuitive and widely accepted view, it can be misleading. The fundamental problem with the workflow view is that products do not actually flow between activities. They flow between organizational functions (or roles)— e.g. lathe operator, inventory control manager, chief executive officer.

The data flow view focuses on how data flow within processes, without making the same mistake as the workflow view. Here, data are seen as moving within and outside processes, between organizational functions. This is one of the reasons why I would recommend the data flow view over other views. Other reasons are its relative simplicity, its long utilization history in computer application development circles, and, finally, its support to understanding of how data flow in organizations. After all, data *is* what *most* flows in organizations, whether we consider organizations that produce or commercialize manufactured goods, information, or services.

Chapter 3

Data, Information and Knowledge

Aren't they the same thing?

We hear the words data, information, and knowledge quite often being used as if they were synonymous. But, are not data, information and knowledge actually the same thing? And, if not, what is the difference? I strongly believe that there are subtle but very important differences among these concepts, and that the nature of these differences is a relatively complex one. Moreover, from a process management perspective, data, information, and knowledge serve entirely different purposes.

The contribution of information technology (IT) providers has perhaps been unmatched in its potential to add to our confusion over the distinction between data and information. Examples can be found in almost any specialized IT publication, conversations with IT company representatives, and even in public speeches by IT "gurus". For example, a senior vice-president of a large software development company was one of the keynote speakers of an international information systems conference in 1995. He referred to the advantages of a well-known commercial group support system in the following terms:

> ...information overflow can be considerably reduced...for example, a few weeks ago I prepared a 2 megabyte report and sent it via electronic mail to ten people. Each of these ten people forwarded a copy of the report to about ten other people...as a result, my report had generated a flow of 200 megabytes of information in the network, in less than four days...

In the example above, the speaker was referring to data, which can be measured in megabytes, as synonymous with information. This can often be misleading, because large sets of data may have very low information content, depending on how well prepared is the receiver of the data to make sense of it. Mistakenly identifying data as information is as commonplace as confusing knowledge with information.

It is curious that the confusion over what information and knowledge are has been nurtured by some of those who are widely recognized as among the forerunners of the study of information and knowledge, and their impact on organizations and society. One the most highly regarded personalities among management consultants and researchers, Claremont Graduate University professor Peter Drucker (1989, pp. 207-208), for example, describes the emergence of the information-based organization in the following terms:

> ...the business, and increasingly the government agency as well, will be *knowledge*-based, composed largely of specialists who direct and discipline their own performance through organized feedback from colleagues and customers. It will be an *information*-based organization...Today's typical organization, in which *knowledge* tends to be concentrated in service staffs perched rather insecurely between top management and the operating people, will likely be labeled a phase, an attempt to infuse *knowledge* from the top rather than obtain *information* from below [my emphasis].

If information and knowledge were the same thing, why use two words when just one would suffice? Even though information and knowledge mean different things to different people, most people use them in different senses. The main reason these two words are often used interchangeably is exactly because there is no agreement over their meaning.

But, who cares? Or, more precisely, why should we worry about the different nature of data, information and knowledge? One reason is because an ocean of data may contain only a small amount of information that is of any value to us, and sifting through this ocean of data may be severely time-consuming (Goldratt, 1991). Another reason is that, without understanding the different nature of these concepts, we cannot fully appreciate how process improvement can contribute to organizational learning, a topic that I discuss in Chapter 4. But there are other reasons, and they relate to the nature of our understanding of the world, or the way we make sense of the world around us.

The world is not only what we perceive it to be through our senses. It is a combination of these perceptions and what is stored in our body, mostly in our brain in the form of neural networks (Callatay, 1986; Dozier, 1992). We can develop our neural networks by interacting with matter and living organisms, notably other human beings. However, in order to interact with other human beings we need to externalize what is stored in our neural networks by means of a code. This code should be understood by other human beings, so communication of what is stored in the form of neural networks can take place.

If data and information were the same, how can the different information content that one e-mail message may have for different recipients be explained? More specifically, let us suppose that an e-mail message written in Spanish (a specific code) is sent to two different recipients. While one of the recipients can read Spanish very well, the other cannot. In this example, the message takes up the same disk space (say, 3.6 kilobytes) on the computers of each of the recipients, which is a measure of the amount of *data* related to the message. Yet, its *information* content is much higher for the recipient who can read Spanish than for the recipient who cannot.

If data and information were the same, then they should not yield different "amounts" when measured for the same object (in this case, the e-mail message in Spanish). It is important to stress that I could have used different terms in this discussion, other than data and information (say, "alpha-stractum" and "capta"). I will stick with the more commonly used terms *data* and *information* in this book, because I believe that the sense in which I have just used these two terms is their most "usual" sense.

The distinction between knowledge and information is a bit more abstract than that between information and data. In order to make this distinction as clear as possible, let us consider the following dialogue between a doctor (D) and her patient (P):

> D: So, what brings you here today?
>
> P: I don't know doctor, I've been feeling a bit strange in the last couple of weeks.
>
> D: What do you mean by "strange"?
>
> P: Burning eyes, stuffed nose...and these things go and come several times a day.
>
> D: Any headaches or fever?
>
> P: No, not at all.
>
> D: Well, we'll run a check up on you, but I think you probably have an allergy.

The patient was feeling the symptoms of what could be an allergy, and therefore he went to see his doctor —an expert who likely *knows* more about medicine than the patient himself. The patient described his symptoms, and the doctor made a tentative diagnosis —"...*you probably have an allergy*..." Is what the patient told the doctor enough for anyone without any medical expertise to come up with the same tentative diagnosis? Well, if this were the case, very few people would agree to pay doctors for consultations. Doctors possess more of something that patients do not have, something typically referred to as *knowledge*, in the specific field of medicine.

Is the nature of the expert knowledge possessed by the doctor, in this case, the same as that of the perception of symptoms experienced by the patient? No, for the simple reason that expert knowledge can be used to generate conclusions based on the description of symptoms—something that the descriptions alone cannot. Therefore, the natures of *descriptions* and *expert knowledge* are different, and it can be shown that none of them is the same as data's. This also suggests that the descriptions are instances of something unique, which I refer to, here, as *information*.

Data are carriers

The usual sense of the term *data*, even if not explicitly stated, is that of carriers of information and knowledge. Data flow in organizational processes between the functions that carry out process activities. This flow takes places through various media, particularly paper, digital electrical impulses (e.g. electronic data interchange systems), analog electrical waves (e.g. telephone), electromagnetic waves (e.g. radio), and air vibrations (e.g. face-to-face conversation). Data can also be stored for later use in different storage media such as magnetic media (e.g. hard and floppy disks), paper, and volatile digital memories (e.g. RAM memory in personal computers).

Data are either transferred or stored through a process of "changing", or generating perturbations on, a given medium. A blank sheet of paper, for example, can be used for data storage (e.g. to write down an address of a friend) or transfer (e.g. to write a memo to an employee) by applying ink on it. Or, from a more business-oriented perspective, if a machine operator wants to tell his supervisor about a problem with a metal-shaping machine, he can approach his supervisor and speak to her face-to-face. In doing so, he uses his vocal cords to generate vibrations in the air (volatile data) that will be received and decoded by the recipient through her hearing organs.

The main point that I want to make here is that data will only become information or knowledge when it is interpreted by human beings (Kryt, 1997), or, in some cases, artificial intelligent agents (see e.g. Russel and Norvig, 1995). As data can be stored and transferred by process functions through applying changes to storage and communication media that will be interpreted by other process functions, we can try an operational definition within the context of process management:

> Let us assume that John performs an organizational function, i.e. he carries out an activity in an organizational process. We can say then that *data* are permanent or volatile changes applied to a communication medium by John to store or transfer information or knowledge. These will later be used by John or someone else (or an artificial intelligent agent) to perform an organizational activity.

The measurement of data depends on the medium used to store or transfer it, as well as on the code used. In most organizational processes, data can be measured in words or symbols, when the medium used is paper, and bits or bytes (one byte is a group of eight bits), when the medium used is a digital one.

In many ways, a bit can be considered the smallest and most fundamental unit of data. It can take only two values: 0 (or false) and 1 (or true). A group of eight bits forms a byte. And, since the number of possible bytes is 2^8 or 256, there can be a direct correspondence between bytes and certain symbols— e.g. the letters of the English and other alphabets. One such set of symbols, largely used to convert alphanumeric characters into bytes and vice-versa, is called the ASCII code (American Standard Code for Information Exchange). Most operating systems in personal computers use the ASCII code, or an extended version of it, to map symbols that have meaning to human beings (e.g. letters and numbers) into bytes stored in any of the computers' data storage devices (e.g. RAM, hard disk, etc.)

Information is descriptive

A hot issue in business circles in the 1990s has been the advent of the "information society," the "information era", and the "information-intensive" organizations. However, any discussion regarding these issues should, of necessity, focus on the nature of information. What is it? Is it a specific kind of entity? If yes, how can we differentiate information from other similar entities? These are core questions in the continuing debate within a number of disciplines such as information systems, management science, engineering, and philosophy. A substantial portion of the literature in these disciplines is devoted to defining information. However, as Budd and Raber (1996, p. 217) note:

> In the course of doing so [i.e. defining information], many aspects of information (technical, physical, semantic, epistemological) are featured as part of the discussion. Part of what emerges is a multifaceted idea and thing that is, at times, defined in terms of what it is not. For instance, information is not merely data; organization and intended meaning transform the bits of data into something that can inform.

From a process-oriented view, information can be seen as carried by data, and as being eminently *descriptive*. From a linguistic perspective, the typical instance of information is the utterance called *assertion*. One example of assertion is: "Today is a sunny day." Independently of what this assertion means exactly (the word "sunny" can mean different things to different people, from sparsely clouded to clear-sky weather), it provides a *description* of the current state of the environment surrounding us. If the environment is seen as an object, the assertion can be seen as defining an attribute of the object, in this case the *weather*, as *sunny*.

Information can be qualified in different ways. It can be more or less complete or accurate, and it can refer to the past, present and future. For example, the assertion "Today is hot!" conveys less accurate information than the assertion "Today's temperature is 85 degrees Fahrenheit." Both assertions describe the present, that is, today. The assertion "The temperature on this day during the last three years has averaged 87 degrees Fahrenheit," provides information about the past. The assertion "Tomorrow the top temperatures will be in the low 90s" provides a description of the future. Although similar to descriptions of the past and the present, descriptions of the future, by their own nature, *always* carry a certain degree of uncertainty.

Knowledge, which will be discussed in more detail in the next section, is often used to generate more information, based on information at hand. The information thereby generated (or *inferred*) is usually not obvious, and therefore possesses some added value in relation to the primary information received as an input by the knowledge holder. One example is the generation of information about the future, e.g. the weather in New York tomorrow, based on information about the present and past, e.g. the weather patterns in New York during the last two years, up to now. This type of information about the future is produced by meteorologists, based on their knowledge about the science of weather forecasting. It is then bought by news services, which in turn broadcast that information to their audiences and, in the process of doing so, manage to make some money out of it.

The value of information

One interesting aspect of information is that its value, that is, how much someone is willing to pay for it and can benefit from it, seems in general to directly correlate some of its attributes. Among these attributes are:

- Its *advanceness*, that is, how much time in advance it describes the future;
- Its *accuracy*, that is, how accurate the description is; and
- Its *completeness*, that is, how complete the description is.

Let me explain the different nature of the attributes above in a business context. The "corporate war" between Coca-Cola and Pepsi in the 1980s was largely one of product differentiation (Ramsey, 1987). Both Coca-Cola and Pepsi tried to increase their shares of the "cola" soft drink market by launching new differentiated (e.g. diet) products ahead of each other. Consider the similar situation of two companies A and B, competing for two million customers in the same industry. Each customer consumes a product supplied by both companies. Analogously to the "cola" war, the product is essentially the same, the main difference being the brand. Each customer consumes 70 units of the product, which costs $3 each, every year, making it a $420 million per year market. Company A has 90 percent of the market, $378 million, while Company B has the other 10 percent, $42 million. Both companies sell with a pre-tax profit margin of 17 percent, which yields approximately $64 million for Company A and $7 million for Company B in absolute pre-tax profits.

Now suppose that Company B decides to launch a new product into the market, whose development time is approximately nine months. The product has the potential to bring Company B's market share up to 20 percent, and send Company A's share down to 80 per cent. This would raise Company B's pre-tax profits up to about $14 million, and make Company A's profits plummet to nearly $57 million. From Company A's perspective (and the value of information always depends on its user and the context in which they are), one piece of information can make a lot of difference—the information that Company B is going to launch a new product. This piece of information can have a high advanceness, if it is provided to Company A well in advance of the product launch, enabling it to take appropriate countermeasures. The same piece of information can have a high accuracy, providing accurate details about the product that is going to be launched, e.g. it might include the precise date of launch. The information can also have high completeness, providing a rich description of the new aspects of the product (e.g. the new flavor, amount of saturated fat, sweetener used etc).

If Company A has no access to information about the new product launch, and, say, obtains some imprecise information a few weeks before the new product is launched, it will have to endure a loss in pre-tax profits of $7 million—this is the worst-case scenario. However, if it gets its hands on accurate and complete information early enough, it can take preventive measures whereby it can at least reduce its losses. For example, if the information is obtained more than 9 months in advance (i.e. has high advanceness), but leaves uncertainty about the characteristics of the product (i.e. has low accuracy and completeness), then Company A might have to develop a range of new products to dampen Company B new product's potential

	Low accuracy And completeness	High accuracy and completeness
High advanceness	Medium value	High value
Low advanceness	Low value	Medium value

Figure 3.1: The value of information

impact on market share. Its profits may still be reduced due to increased product development costs.

Having access to detailed information about Company B's new product (i.e. highly accurate and complete information) only four months before the launch (i.e. low advanceness information) may lead to a similar end result. That is, Company A may be able to develop an intermediary product that will reduce Company B new launch's impact on market share.

The best scenario is perhaps that in which Company A has access to highly detailed information (i.e. highly accurate and complete information) about Company B's new launch early enough (i.e. the information has high advanceness) so it can develop a similar new product and get it out into the market before Company B does. According to our initial assumptions, this could potentially bring Company A's market share up to 95 percent and increase profits in about $4 million.

In the example above, no information or information with low accuracy, completeness, or advanceness, would be of low value to Company A. Information with high accuracy and completeness, but low advanceness, (or vice versa) would have a medium value, as it could prevent a loss of $7 million in pre-tax profits a year. Finally, information with high accuracy, completeness, and advanceness would have a high value, enabling an increase in profits of $4 million a year. This relationship between information value and its attributes is illustrated in Figure 3.1.

Although the example above is concerned with a decision making process at the strategic level, we can extrapolate the relationship between information value and the attributes of advanceness and accuracy to most organizational processes. Simply put, process-related information seems to be an important enabling factor for the members of a process team (that is, those who perform process activities) to do their job efficiently and effectively, whatever the process is.

Knowledge is associative

While information is eminently descriptive, and can refer to the past, present and future, knowledge is by its own nature eminently *associative*. That is, it allows us to "associate" different world states and respective mental representations, which are typically linked to or described by means of pieces of information (i.e. knowledge allows us to link different pieces of information, and make decisions based on that). The associative aspect of knowledge can be seen as being of two types, namely correlational and causal, which are in turn only two types of what has been referred to by Weick and Bougon (1986, p. 104) as "cognitive archetypes." And, again, knowledge can be directly stored by human beings through neural connections, which in turn are concentrated mostly in the brain. If someone loses part of her brain, she may also lose part of the knowledge previously stored there in the form of neural connections.

Correlational knowledge usually connects two or more pieces of information that describe events or situations that have happened, are happening, or will happen at the *same* time. Causal knowledge connects pieces of information that describe the state of the world at *different* times. For example, consider the associative knowledge represented in the following decision rule: "If John has a some fever and is sneezing, then John has likely a cold." The knowledge embodied in this decision rule is of the correlational type, because it affirms that someone who has fever and sneezing is in fact displaying typical cold symptoms—that is, "fever", "sneezing" and "cold" typically happen at the same time.

Another example, now of a different type of knowledge, is provided by the rule "if John smokes a lot, then he will probably die from lung cancer." This decision rule expresses causal knowledge. As such, the rule connects two events that take place at different times: John smoking a lot, in the present, and John dying of lung cancer, in the future. It is to causal knowledge that Dennett (1991, p. 144) refers, when he claims that:

> The brain's task is to guide the body it controls through a world of shifting conditions and sudden surprises, so it must gather information from that world and use *swiftly* to "produce future"— to extract anticipations in order to stay one step ahead of disaster [original emphasis].

Knowledge drives the flow of myriad decisions that have to be made even in the simplest organizational processes. Steel plants, for example, rely on process teams to load and operate smelters. Consider the predictive knowledge expressed in the rule "if the smelter is set at a temperature of 3,000 degrees Celsius, then a one-ton load of steel will be smelted in 43 minutes." This is one of the pieces of knowledge that allow a smelter operator to predict that a batch of solid steel weighing about one ton will be in liquid form approximately 43 minutes after it is loaded into the smelter, if the smelter is set properly. This prediction allows the smelter operator to program a stop in the smelting process at the right time and let the liquid steel flow out of the smelter, which saves energy and, at the same time, prevents the steel from overcooking.

In order for teamwork to yield effective and efficient outcomes, those who perform activities in a process must share predictive knowledge. In the example, those who use the steel in liquid form for shaping steel parts should ideally hold at least part of the knowledge held by the smelter operator. If they know of the "forty-three-minute rule," they can also predict that a batch of steel will be ready within 43 minutes from the time it is loaded in solid form, and have their own equipment prepared at the right time to work on the liquid steel.

In business in general, knowledge seems to be inextricably linked with decision-making (Olson and Courtney, 1992; Holsapple and Whinston, 1996), perhaps because one of the best ways of assessing the actual value of knowledge is through the assessment of the outcomes of decisions made based on it. Holsapple and Whinston (1996, p. 6) talk of the importance of knowledge for decision-making:

> For centuries, managers have used the *knowledge* available to them to make *decisions* [original emphasis] shaping the world in which they lived. The impacts of managers' decisions have ranged from those affecting the world in some small or fleeting way to those of global and lasting proportions. Over the centuries, the number of decisions being made per time period has tended to increase. The complexity of decision activities has grown. The amount of knowledge used in making decisions has exploded. There is no sign that these trends are about to stop. If anything, they appear to be accelerating.

Knowledge has been distinguished from information and also linked with decision-making in different fields of research and academic disciplines. In the field of artificial intelligence, for example, information has been typically represented through "facts". Knowledge, on the other hand, has been expressed by means of a number of different representations, such as semantic networks, frames, scripts, neural networks, and production rules; the latter being the most common in practical knowledge-based computer systems (Callatay, 1986; Holyoak, 1991; Olson and Courtney, 1992). Production rules are conditional statements in *if-then* form, like the ones used to exemplify knowledge in this section.

In the fields of psychology and social cognition, knowledge has been expressed through schemas (Lord and Foti, 1986) and cognitive maps (Weick and Bougon, 1986). These are in turn seen as guiding individual and group behavior, and using as input environmental stimuli obtained through the senses. The concept of schema was developed as a reaction to studies of memory pioneered by Ebbingaus, which made use of arbitrary materials and sensorial stimuli to determine factors that influence the formation of memory and recall of information (Gardner, 1985). The development of the concept of schema is credited to Bartlett (1932), who used an Indian folk tale called "The War of the Ghosts" to show that existing mental structures strongly influenced memory formation and recall. Such existing mental structures, which were used by Bartlett's study subjects to process of information coming from the tale, were called schemas. Essentially, Bartlett has shown that individuals possessing different schemas would interpret the tale, which is filled with strange gaps and bizarre causal sequences, in substantially different ways.

In biology in general, and, more particularly, in neurology, knowledge is typically seen as associated with long-term nerve-based memory structures whose main goal is information processing (Pinker, 1997). Information is seen as usually associated with short-term neural connections that appear to "vanish" from conscious memory after a while. For example, the knowledge of how to operate a telephone is stored in long-term memory structures, whereas the information represented by a phone number is stored in short-term memory structures.

The value of knowledge

Knowledge is usually much more expensive to produce than information. For example, information in the form of mutual fund indicators (e.g. weekly earnings, monthly price fluctuation) is produced by means of little more than simple calculations performed on data about share prices and their fluctuation over a time period. The knowledge of how mutual fund indicators fluctuate, however, requires years of analysis of *information* to be built. This analysis of information leads to the development of knowledge that allows an expert investor to select the best mutual funds on which to invest her money given the configuration of the economy. This leads us to the question: How is knowledge produced?

Comparative studies of experts and non-experts suggest that expertise is usually acquired through an inductive process in which generalizations are made based on the frequency with which a certain piece of information occurs. These generalizations are the basis for the construction of knowledge (Camerer and Johnson, 1991).

A different and less common method used to generate knowledge is deduction, whereby hidden knowledge is produced based on existing knowledge through a set of logical steps (Teichman and Evans, 1995). This method has been used in the development of a large body of knowledge in the form of "theorems", particularly in the fields of mathematics and theoretical physics (Hawking, 1988).

An example of knowledge building through induction is that undergone by novice investors in the stock market. The observation that shares of a small number of companies in high technology industries have risen ten percentage points above the Standard & Poor's 500 average index during a period of six months may prompt a novice investor to put all of her money into these shares. A professional investor, however, knows, based on, say, ten years of experience as a broker in the stock market, that a six-month observation period is not long enough to support such a risky decision, and opts for a more diversified portfolio. In cases such as these, the novice investor will eventually lose money, particularly because her decision to sell will probably follow the same pattern as her decision to buy. It will be based on inferences based on a time span that is too short, leading her to buy shares that are overvalued and sell these shares when they are undervalued. According to Boroson (1997), most non-professional investors follow this recipe, which in most cases leads to disastrous consequences.

The example above illustrates a key finding from research on cognitive psychology: People usually tend to infer knowledge based on the observation of a small number of events, that is, on limited information (Feldman, 1986). Moreover, once knowledge structures are developed, changing these structures can become more difficult than developing them from scratch (Woofford, 1994). A conversation that I recently had with a university colleague illustrates these cognitive biases. My colleague had gone to two different agencies of the New Jersey Motor Vehicle Services where he met employees who lacked sympathy and friendliness. He also had gone to a similar agency in the state of Pennsylvania, whose employees he found to be very nice. Later, during a chat with friends he said that:

...All MVS employees in New Jersey are very grumpy, difficulty to deal with...The state of Pennsylvannia is much better in that respect...

I pointed out that he had just made a gross generalization, given the small sample of MVS agencies visited—two in New Jersey and one in Pennsylvania only.

Although he agreed with me, he was nevertheless adamant that he would never go to a New Jersey MVS agency again, unless it was absolutely necessary. If this was the case, he said he would ask a less "touchy" person to go— his wife.

The development of theories of knowledge (or epistemologies) and scientific methods of inquiry has been motivated by a need to overcome cognitive biases such as those illustrated above. This has been one of the main common goals of such thinkers as Aristotle, René Descartes, Gottlob Frege, Bertrand Russell, Karl Popper, and Thomas Kuhn. Epistemologies and scientific methods have provided a basis for the conduct of research in general, and in consequence for technological advances that have shaped organizations and society. Every year, hundreds of billions of dollars are invested in research, with the ultimate goal of generating highly reliable and valid knowledge. And the market value of organizations is increasingly assessed based on the amount of knowledge that they possess, rather than on their material assets base (Davidow and Malone, 1992; Toffler, 1991).

Paul Strassmann, a former information technology executive at companies such as Xerox, Kraft Foods, and the US Department of Defense, suggests that variations in the perceptions of organizational knowledge account for the growing trend toward overvaluing, or undervaluing stocks in the share market. According to Strassmann, the perception that a stock is overvalued stems from the failure of current accounting systems to account for the knowledge assets of organizations, and he presents an impressive array of data to support this idea. Abbott Laboratories is one of the companies he used to illustrate this point.

Over a period of seven years from 1987 to 1994, the ratio between Abbott's market value (defined by stock price) and its equity has swung from five up to nearly eight and back down to about seven. However, the ratio between market value and "equity plus knowledge assets" remained almost constant over that period, smoothly gravitating around two. This supports Strassmann's (1997, p. 13) position that the market perceives the accumulation of knowledge assets, which is reflected in the high correlation between share prices of organizations and their knowledge assets, even though the knowledge assets are not shown on a company's balance sheet:

> The sustained stability of the market-to-capital ratio which accounts for the steady rise in the knowledge capital of Abbott Laboratories confirms that the stock market will recognize the accumulation of knowledge as an asset even though the accountants do not. The stock market will also reward the accumulators of knowledge capital because investors recognize that the worth of a corporation is largely in its management, not its physical of financial assets.

When we move from a macroeconomic to a microeconomic perspective, and look at the business processes of a firm, the trend toward valuing knowledge seems to be similar to the one just described. Knowledge allows for the prediction of process-related outcomes, from the more general prediction of a group of customers' acceptance of a new product, to much more specific predictions, such as slight manual corrections needed on a computer board surface after it goes through an automatic drill. Correlational knowledge enables process-control workstation operators at a chemical plant to link a sudden rise of an acidity gauge to an incorrect setting of the flow through a pipe valve. This enables the operators to take the appropriate measures to bring the acidity level down to normal.

The workers who hold bodies of expert knowledge are rewarded according to their ability to use them to perform process activities in an efficient and effective way. This is typically done through linking different types of information, which can be done through formal education or personal experience (i.e. the building mental knowledge bases), and generating information about the future based on information about the past or present (i.e. predicting the future). Organizational wealth is closely linked to the ability to build and use technological artifacts to control future states of the (economic, physical) environment in which organizations operate. However, this control is impossible without the related ability to predict the future, which in turn relies heavily on predictive knowledge.

Organizational knowledge is believed to be the single most important factor that ultimately defines the ability of a company to survive and thrive in a competitive environment (Davidow and Malone, 1992; Drucker, 1995). This knowledge is probably stored mostly in the brains of the workers of an organization, although it may also be stored in computer systems and databases (Alster, 1997; Strassmann, 1996; 1997), and other archival records (e.g. printed reports).

Whatever form it takes, knowledge is a commodity. And, as such, it can be bought and sold, which makes its value fluctuate more or less according to the laws that regulate supply and demand. Abundant knowledge, which can be represented by a large number of available professionals with the same type of expertise, becomes cheap when supply surpasses demand, which is typically reflected in a decrease in the salaries of some groups of professionals. One the other hand, a situation in which some types of highly specialized knowledge are in short supply, while demand grows sharply in a short period of time, can lead the knowledge holders to be caught by surprise when faced with unusually high bids from employers. For example, Web Java programmers were being offered salaries of up to $170,000 early in 1996, even though the demand for their new expertise was virtually nil until 1995. This was the year Java was first released by Sun Microsystems; two years after the University of Illinois began the distribution of its World Wide Web browser Mosaic.

Linking data, information and knowledge

Although they are different conceptual entities, data, information and knowledge are inextricably connected. This may be one of the reasons why they are so often confused. As discussed before, data are perturbations on a communication or storage medium that are used to transfer or store information and knowledge. Therefore, knowledge and information can be neither communicated nor stored without data.

Information is used to describe the world, and can provide a description of the past, present and future (information about the future always carries a certain degree of uncertainty). Correlational knowledge allows for the linking of different pieces of information about the present. In this case, usually some of the information pieces are obvious and used as a departure point and the other pieces are hidden and allow for relevant decisions. Predictive knowledge enables the production of information about the future, typically based on information about the past and the present. That is, information is generated based on both correlational and predictive knowledge.

However, the reverse relationship is also valid, that is, knowledge can be generated based on information. In fact, the main means by which reliable knowledge is produced is the systematic analysis of information about the past. This analysis typically leads to the observation of patterns that are combined into predictive and associative rules (i.e. knowledge).

Consider, for example, the following case involving Hopper Specialty and NCR (Geyelin, 1994). In 1987, Hopper Specialty, a retail vendor of industrial hardware in Farmington, New Mexico, decided to purchase a computerized inventory management system from NCR, a large developer of computer hardware and software, headquartered in Dayton, Ohio. The system in question was called Warehouse Manager, and was installed in 1988. Several problems surfaced immediately after the system had been installed.

According to Hopper Specialty's representatives the system never worked as it was supposed to, displaying an assortment of problems such as extremely low response times, constant locking up of terminals, and corrupted data files. In 1993, more than five years after the system was installed, Hopper Specialty cancelled the contract with NCR and sued the company, claiming that it had suffered a loss of $4.2 million in profits due to problems caused by the installation and use of Warehouse Manager. NCR's lawyers immediately asked that the lawsuit be dismissed on the grounds that it was filed too late—New Mexico's statute of limitations for this type of lawsuit is only four years.

Ethical considerations aside, NCR's lawyers had access to information and knowledge that allowed them to safely move for a case dismissal. The information to which I refer here regards New Mexico's statute of limitations, and can be expressed by the assertion: "In New Mexico, a law suit such as the one filed by Hopper Specialty should be filed within at least four years after the alleged breach of contract occurs." The knowledge possessed by NCR's lawyers allowed them to build a link between information about the law, in this case the statute of limitations, and the likely consequence (information about the future) of grounding their defense on New Mexico's statute of limitations. This knowledge can be summarily expressed by the rule: "*If* we move for a case dismissal based on New Mexico's statute of limitations, *then* it is likely that the case will be quickly dismissed by the judge presiding the case."

Figure 3.2 depicts the relationship between data, information, and knowledge based on the case discussed above. The following printed or electronic documents store information that could be used by NCR's lawyers to defend their company in the lawsuit filed by Hopper:

- The lawsuit notification;
- The contract between NCR & Hopper;
- Warehouse Manager's documentation;
- A legal database of previous cases;
- Law books; and
- New Mexico's constitution.

The above items are physical or electronic records, i.e. data, which had first had to be read by NCR's lawyers, so they (i.e. the lawyers) could extract some pieces of

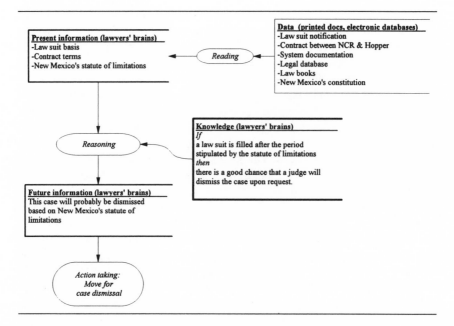

Figure 3.2: The relationship between data, information and knowledge

relevant present information (i.e. information about the present situation). Examples of such pieces of relevant information are the terms of the contract between NCR and Hopper, and New Mexico's statute of limitations.

Present information can then be combined with knowledge linking the main goal of a generic statute of limitations and the likely consequences of anyone not observing the lawsuit filing expiry period stipulated by it. This combination of knowledge and information allows for the prediction of the future with a certain degree of certainty, that is, the generation of "future information", or information about the future. In the case of NCR versus Hopper, this future information was the prediction that the presiding judge would dismiss the case based on New Mexico's statute of limitations. NCR's lawyers therefore took the appropriate action of moving for a case dismissal.

Summary and concluding remarks

There is generalized confusion about the concepts of data, information, and knowledge. This is largely fueled by disparate meanings assigned by diverse academic disciplines and industry groups to these terms. Although many use the three words as synonymous, there are subtle and relevant differences among data, information and knowledge.

Data are carriers of information and knowledge. Information and knowledge are coded into data so they can be either synchronously communicated (i.e. communicated in a situation where both sender and receiver interact at the same time) or stored for future use. This can be done by the same person who generated the data, or by other people. In the latter case, data is used for asynchronous communication. In organizations, data flow between functions that carry out process activities. Such flow can take place through various media, particularly paper, digital electrical impulses (e.g. electronic data interchange systems), analog electrical waves (e.g. telephone), electromagnetic waves (e.g. radio), and air vibrations (e.g. face-to-face conversation). Data can also be stored for later use in different storage media such as magnetic media (e.g. hard and floppy disks), paper, and volatile digital memories (e.g. RAM memory in personal computers).

Information is predominantly descriptive, and refers to the past, present, and future. While information about the past and present can be completely accurate, information about the future is always inherently uncertain. The most typical instance of information is the linguistic construct known as *assertion*, which has the general form *object-verb-attribute*. One example of assertion is "Today is a sunny day," where the object is "today's weather," the verb is "is," and the attribute is "sunny."

Unlike information, knowledge is chiefly associative. That is, it defines associations between pieces of generic of specific information, so "hidden" information instances can be inferred from information at hand. Knowledge associations can be correlational or causal. Correlational knowledge associations link two or more pieces of information related to same-time events. Causal knowledge links information instances that relate to different-time events.

The economic value of both information and knowledge can be estimated based on the decisions made based on them. Information's value varies according to a number of attributes, including its accuracy, completeness, and advanceness (i.e. how much time it is obtained before the event to which it refers occurs). The economic value of knowledge is more difficult to estimate. And, given the fact that knowledge is harder to acquire than information, it is reasonable to speculate that, when compared with information in the same terms, its economic value will be usually higher.

Evidence suggests that people who perform specialized functions in the same organizational process should share a certain percentage of their individual knowledge. Although many formidable obstacles to process-related knowledge sharing exist, it is an important ingredient in productivity and quality optimization.

Chapter 4

Process Improvement and Knowledge Communication

Organizational knowledge and competitiveness

As we have seen in Chapter 3, knowledge, whether stored in the brain or in computer databases, is necessary for the processing of information. Information processing, in turn, has been identified as the main reason why organizations exist[1] (Galbraith, 1973). That is, purposeful organization of people, capital, and other resources is necessary so information processing can be done efficiently and effectively. Information processing, in turn, is seen as a fundamental step in the generation and delivery of products and services by organizations to their customers.

Given the prominent role that information processing seems to play in organizational processes, and the assumption that information processing relies heavily on knowledge, the frequent claims that the collective knowledge held by organizations is the single most important factor defining their competitiveness do not seem unreasonable. The amount of relevant shared knowledge among individuals in process teams has been linked to the efficiency and effectiveness of such teams (Boland and Tenkasi, 1995; Nelson and Cooprider, 1996; Nosek and McNeese, 1997). Shared team knowledge has been equated to higher flexibility of organizational processes, as it can reduce the need for bureaucratic and automated procedures to mechanize and standardize procedures (Davidow and Malone, 1992). That is, more shared knowledge among team members may reduce the need for workflow control and automation.

But, what is organizational knowledge, and how is it related to team knowledge? Knowledge exists in organizations in a dispersed way, and is predominantly held by the individuals who perform process activities. A new concept that tries to expand the locus of knowledge, from the individual towards the group, is the concept of *team* knowledge (Katzenbach and Smith, 1993). Team knowledge is defined as the collective knowledge possessed by groups of individuals involved in the execution of organizational processes, regardless of process scope. Such processes can be as diverse as the processes of *home loan approval* and *hamburger preparation*.

An even higher level concept has been created to refer to the collective knowledge of an organization, namely *organizational* knowledge or "knowledge of the firm" (Kogut and Zander, 1992), which can be defined as the combined knowledge of the various process teams that make up an organization. Part of this collective knowledge can also be stored in data storage devices, often as components of computer-based systems (Strassman, 1996).

The need for knowledge sharing

Due to its associative nature, the continuous build up and intensive use of knowledge is a necessity in a complex society. Here, the term "complexity" implies a large number of associations or interdependencies, whether we look at society from an environmental, artifact-oriented, sociological, psychological, or any other relevant perspective (Stacey, 1995; Gleick, 1993; Lewin, 1993).

Knowledge creation feeds complexity and vice-versa (Probst and Buchel, 1997), in what could be seen as an open-ended spiral. For example, new discoveries about a terminal disease and its genetic roots can trigger the development of new technologies and drugs for treatment and prevention of the disease. This in turn can lead to the development of new equipment, and, on a different scale, new drug manufacturing companies. New governmental market regulations may follow. New militant groups fighting for their rights may emerge as those who have the genes that cause the disease organize themselves against possible discrimination by insurance companies. New research fields, theories, and academic disciplines may be spawn.

As knowledge becomes more voluminous and complex, so does the need for knowledge specialization by individuals. Through formal and informal education as well as practice, experts in fields as diverse as accounting and medicine absorb and use specialized knowledge that is not held by large sections of the population in general. The market rewards knowledge specialization and expertise through higher paying jobs and social status.

Obstacles, particularly in the form of time constraints, prevent individuals from becoming experts in several different knowledge specialties at the same time. For example, earlier studies by Simon and Chase (1973) suggest that a chess player cannot reach the grandmaster level in fewer than nine or ten years, regardless of how hard she tries and how intelligent she is.

A large and highly educated mass of people spanning many countries ensures that knowledge is created at a very fast rate so as to push individuals into focusing their cognitive efforts onto narrow fields of expertise.

As knowledge becomes more specialized, so does the need for information and knowledge sharing, which can be achieved through oral and written communication among those who possess different pieces of specialized knowledge. This need is motivated by the fact that even though knowledge has grown very specialized (or precisely because of it), most processes in society require the engagement of several individuals, each of them contributing their own expert knowledge. In organizations as well as in society in general, knowledge to carry out processes is not found in concentrated form. As Hayek (1996, p. 7) points out in his seminal article *The Use of Knowledge in Society*:

The peculiar character of the problem of a rational economic order is determined precisely by the fact that the knowledge of the circumstances which we must use never exists in concentrated or integrated form but solely as the dispersed bits of incomplete and frequently contradictory knowledge which separate individuals possess.

An analysis of the shop floor of two automobile manufacturers provides a good illustration of the distributed nature of knowledge. Volkswagen and Ford's plants in Sao Paulo manufactured several car models. Although Volkswagen and Ford usually designed each of the models assembled in their plants, most of the parts that went into the models came from their suppliers, which could easily amount to several hundreds for each automobile manufacturer. Breaks, engine parts, or even something as simple as an exhaust pipe or a seat belt, were individually obtained from different suppliers and assembled into a car by the auto-makers.

Among the reasons why outsourcing the manufacturing of car parts was more economical for Volkswagen and Ford than making those parts in-house, was that the cost of keeping and managing the specialized knowledge that went into economically and effectively building each car part was too high.

Outsourcing pushes the responsibility of keeping and managing part-specific knowledge to the supplier. But, although the knowledge that goes into manufacturing each car part is largely possessed by the supplier, Volkswagen and Ford's engineers need to hold part of it in order to design their cars. For example, they need to know whether an airbag, which is manufactured elsewhere, will inflate properly if they reduce the size of the airbag's compartment. That is, sharing knowledge becomes a necessity if the automobile manufacturers and their suppliers are to build low cost cars that meet car buyers' expectations. And such expectations are likely to be increasingly inflated in a highly competitive marketplace such as that of the 1990s and beyond.

Organizational learning and knowledge transfer

The example of the automobile manufacturers in the previous section highlights the need for knowledge sharing between different organizations; the manufacturers themselves and their suppliers, in the case. One management movement has consistently argued for the development of knowledge creation and sharing capabilities within *and* between organizations as a fundamental step towards achieving heightened competitiveness. This management movement is the *learning organizations* movement (Garratt, 1994; Kofman and Senge, 1993; Senge et al., 1994).

In order to foster knowledge creation and sharing, it is argued that learning organizations should establish an organizational culture that is conducive to these. A climate of risk-taking and experimentation has been found to be an important factor in establishing such organizational culture (Senge, 1990). Such climate can be achieved through the adoption of new management practices and paradigms that stimulate creativity and proactive behavior (Nevis et al., 1995), as well as social interaction (Roskelly, 1994).

In spite of attempts to create organizational cultures conducive to learning, the transferring of acquired knowledge from one part of an organization to another remains a complex and problematic issue (CHE, 1995). This is particularly unfortunate, as transfer of acquired knowledge across different organizational areas has been itself presented as one of the most important components of organizational learning (Redding and Catalanello, 1994) and competitiveness (Boland and Tenkasi, 1995).

Types of exchanges in organizational processes

Given the relatively high significance placed on inter-functional knowledge communication as a component of organizational learning, the search for ways to improve this communication is warranted. In order to do so, it is important to understand knowledge communication from a product exchange perspective. Such perspective takes into consideration the exchanges of tangible (e.g. parts, materials) and intangible (e.g. information, knowledge) elements between organizational functions (or roles).

Inter-functional exchanges in processes can be seen as being of two main types, namely material and data exchanges. As mentioned before, there have been repeated claims, particularly since the 1970s, that we are now living in an information (or symbolic) society (Toffler, 1970; 1991). To these, were added claims that we are in the midst of an information explosion where more and more people are working in the "information sector" (Hirschheim, 1985), and that organizations have become "information organizations" (Drucker, 1989).

As a result of these claims, I have been long since curious as to the extent to which information-bearing exchanges (i.e. exchanges of data) outweigh material exchanges in organizations. This curiosity led, in 1996, to a study of 15 business processes in three organizations. A description of each process is provided in Table 4.1, along with the name of the organization where each process was located.

One of the organizations from which process-related data were obtained was Westaflex, an international car parts manufacturer based in southern Brazil. The other two organizations were based in New Zealand. One was Waikato University, whose main campus was based in the city of Hamilton, and the other was MAF Quality Management, a semi-autonomous branch of the New Zealand Ministry of Agriculture and Fisheries with offices spread throughout the country.

The study of the processes involved the identification of data and material exchanges between the organizational functions that performed activities in each process. Overall, 123 exchanges were identified. One hundred and three of these exchanges were found to be data exchanges, which amounts to approximately 84 percent. Only 20 of these exchanges were found to be material exchanges, approximately 16 percent. The distribution of these exchanges according to type (i.e. data or material) is illustrated in Figure 4.1.

The number of data exchanges was over five times that of material exchanges. Although the sample of business processes analyzed was small (i.e. 15), the large contrast between the quantity of data and material exchanges and the fact that the sample was obtained from three different organizations suggests that such contrast may be found in other organizations. Moreover, nearly half of the processes studied came from Westaflex, a manufacturing organization. Thus, one can reasonably expect the proportion of data exchanges to be even higher in organizations outside the manufacturing sector.

Process description	Organization
Product design	Westaflex
Parts manufacturing	Westaflex
Order delivery	Westaflex
Raw material purchase	Westaflex
University course preparation	Waikato University
University course teaching	Waikato University
Communication of a pest/disease outbreak	MAF Quality Management
Quality management consulting	MAF Quality Management
Quality inspection of parts/materials	Westaflex
Plant machinery maintenance	Westaflex
Equipment adaptation for new product	Westaflex
Software support for users	MAF Quality Management
Internal newspaper editing	MAF Quality Management
IT users support	MAF Quality Management
Staff training and development	MAF Quality Management

Table 4.1: Organizational processes studied

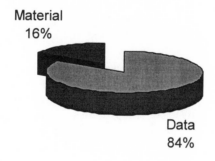

Figure 4.1: Distribution of exchanges according to their type

Process improvement and knowledge communication

In Chapter 3 the idea that data can be seen as carriers of information and knowledge was proposed. I also pointed out that information is predominantly descriptive, whereas knowledge is predominantly associative. Information allows us to describe the world through assertive statements about it, such as, "Today it is going to rain!" Knowledge allows us to associate different assertions that can occur at the same time or at different points in time, such as in "If today it is going to rain, then the road is going to be wet."

I also noted in Chapter 2 that process improvement has been at the heart of what is often referred as organizational learning, particularly regarding the concept of double-loop learning proposed by Argyris (1977; 1992). However, hard evidence that empirically suggests that process improvement is in some way causally linked with organizational learning has been very scarce, practically nonexistent.

If we look at the set of processes described in the previous section, we can see that they can provide *the basis* for showing that process improvement can lead to organizational learning. For this to happen, however, a control group of *improvement* processes is needed. The reason is simple, the 15 processes studied are all routine core and support processes in the organizations they were taken from. None of them is an *improvement* process.

Improvement processes are usually *group* (or team) processes, whereby business processes are analyzed and redesigned for improvement. An example of an improvement process is MetaProi, which stands for Meta-Process for Process Improvement. MetaProi is called a *meta*-process because it is itself a process and yet it is used for improving other processes[2]. MetaProi is described in detail in Appendix A.

Since none of the processes described in the previous section is an improvement process, a comparison between these processes and a new set of improvement processes could shed some light onto the different nature of *improvement* and *routine* processes regarding knowledge and information communication. It would have been even better if the new set of improvement processes could be obtained from the same three organizations mentioned in the previous section, so organizational "culture" and other organization-specific factors could be eliminated as possible sources of bias in the analysis.

Data could not be obtained from improvement processes at Westaflex, but I was able to collect data from the other two organizations. Twelve improvement processes (or meta-processes) conducted at MAF Quality Management and Waikato University by process improvement groups were analyzed, and then compared to the 15 routine core and support processes described in the previous section. A description of these processes is provided in Table 4.2. Groups conducted process improvement activities according to MetaProi's guidelines (see Appendix A).

Different communication channels have been used during the discussions. Group communication took place predominantly through an e-mail conferencing system (developed by me using Novell Groupwise[3] macros), face-to-face meetings, and phone conversations. The e-mail conferencing system allowed members to send e-mail messages to a central mailbox, which then automatically distributed the messages to all the other members of the group (e.g. as in Internet e-mail lists, a.k.a. *Listservs*). Typically, group members were physically dispersed, either in different offices of the same building or campus, or across different cities or campuses. Most group members were drawn from the same process team, that is, they were involved in the execution of the same (typically interdepartmental) process.

I analyzed discrete and written exchanges of data (e.g. forms, reports, e-mail messages, memos, faxes etc.) in both groups of processes (i.e. routine and improvement processes). In doing so, I was particularly concerned with identifying information and knowledge occurrences in each of these exchanges. I did so consistently with the operational definitions of knowledge and information, discussed in Chapter

Process description	Organization
University course improvement	Waikato University
Undergraduate academic support improvement	Waikato University
Student computer support improvement	Waikato University
Student assignment handling improvement	Waikato University
International graduate student support improvement	Waikato University
International student adaptation support improvement	Waikato University
Software support improvement	MAF Quality Management
Newsletter editing improvement	MAF Quality Management
Pest/disease outbreak communication improvement	MAF Quality Management
Quality management consulting improvement	MAF Quality Management
IT users support improvement	MAF Quality Management
Staff training and development improvement	MAF Quality Management

Table 4.2: Improvement processes studied

3. A given data exchange was seen as carrying information if it had at least one purely descriptive statement. Such statements were identified by the presence of isolated *object-verb-attribute* sequences, without any associative (either causal or correlational) reference. Examples of these are "John is in Singapore this week," "Our cycle time has increased 20 percent in comparison with the same quarter last year," and "Our sales figures always go down at this time of the year.".

A given data exchange was seen as carrying knowledge if it had at least one associative statement that could be expressed as an *if-then* statement. Associative statements are those which associate different pieces of information in a causal or correlational way. These associations can be more or less general (or specific). General associations express knowledge in a relatively generic way. For example, consider the following statement: "I think that increased instances of litigation have been caused by our lack of understanding of our customers' needs." This statement carries knowledge that is relatively generic, because it associates two *classes* of phenomena "increased instances of litigation" with a "lack of understanding of customer needs". Specific associations express knowledge in a relatively specific context. Consider the statement: "The reluctance of our chief operations officer was the main reason why our re-engineering project failed." This is a much more specific statement insofar as it associates two specific *instances* of phenomena, namely "the reluctance of a specific organization function" and "the failure of a specific re-engineering project."

The absolute counts of knowledge and information exchanges across different process types (i.e. routine and improvement processes) are shown in Figure 4.2. There are a few important points to be made based on these aggregate numbers.

- There were considerably fewer data exchanges that carried knowledge in comparison to those that carried only information.
- Almost all data exchanges carried information. Only two data exchanges in improvement processes did not carry any information (these exchanges did not carry any knowledge either). This makes sense, as at least "something" (i.e. some knowledge of information) is meant to be transferred in data exchanges

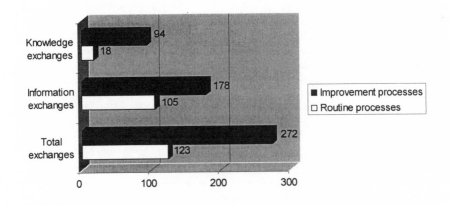

Figure 4.2: Knowledge and information flowing across different types of processes

anyhow, otherwise they would never happen in the first place.

The number of knowledge-bearing exchanges in improvement processes (94) was much higher than in routine processes (18), in spite of the fact that more routine processes than improvement process were analyzed. Remember that 15 routine processes were compared with only 12 improvement processes.

Even though the number of knowledge-bearing exchanges in improvement processes was higher than that found in routine processes, a careful analysis has to account (an control) for the fact that there were more data exchanges in improvement processes than in routine processes. That is, process improvement group members exchanged more data than members of teams performing routine processes.

If there were more data exchanges in improvement processes, then it is reasonable to expect that there would be more knowledge exchanges, even if the ratio between knowledge-bearing exchanges and total exchanges is the same for improvement and routine processes. In this sense, the comparison of the figures—ninety-four obtained for the improvement processes and 18 obtained for the routine processes—may not be a totally fair one. Nevertheless, this comparison indicates that process improvement leads to an increase, in absolute terms, in knowledge exchanges in organizations.

What is needed to complete a careful analysis is to find out what the percentage of knowledge-bearing exchanges is when all exchanges are considered. This normalized figure gives an idea of how much knowledge there is *per data exchange* in improvement as well as routine processes.

Figure 4.3, shows the normalized knowledge content per data exchange for improvement and routine processes, which was obtained by dividing the number of knowledge-bearing exchanges by the total number of exchanges for each process type. The percentages shown, 34 and 14 percent, suggest a much higher knowledge content in data exchanges taking place in improvement processes than in those

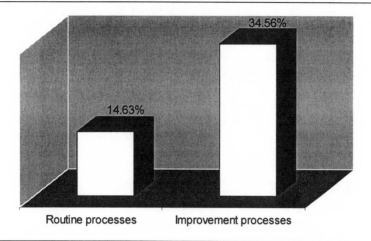

Figure 4.3: Normalized knowledge content per exchange across process types

observed in routine processes.

In the face of the analysis of knowledge and information exchanges discussed above, one may argue that no conclusions can be made about knowledge and information *communication* patterns. The reason is because I cannot be sure that the knowledge and information extracted from the data exchanges would *actually be transferred* between the originator of each data exchange and its recipient. In other words, the fact that knowledge and information are apparently being exchanged (according to my analysis) does not mean that they are being actually *communicated*. My answer to this is based on one important, and in my view sound, assumption, which is that decreases in *communication fidelity* should occur uniformly across the sample of exchanges analyzed.

What I mean by *communication fidelity*, is the ratio between what is exchanged and what is really communicated. Communication fidelity can be reduced by many factors, such as:

- Different types of "noise," that is, extraneous elements that distort the meaning of what is meant to be communicated;
- Lack of a shared understanding of the language used for communication; or
- Lack of interest in the topic about which information or knowledge is being communicated.

My point is that if communication fidelity is reduced, it is reasonable to expect that such reduction will take place in more or less the same way throughout the routine and improvement processes studied. Since my conclusions are based on the comparison of figures obtained for each of these types of processes, they should be uniformly affected by a possible reduction in communication fidelity. Such reduction could be seen as a multiplicative factor f that would be equally applied to improvement and routine process variables. Whenever relative considerations are made, f would automatically be cancelled out. For example, if f was .5, the percentages in Figure 4.3 would have been *26.11 percent* for improvement processes, and *8.57 percent* for routine processes. That would not alter the fact that the relative knowledge content of data exchanges in improvement processes is much higher than that found in routine processes, which is one of the main findings of my analysis.

One of the main conclusions that can be inferred from the results presented here is that process improvement fosters knowledge communication. And, since knowledge communication is an important component of organizational learning, then it follows that process improvement fosters organization learning.

Summary and concluding remarks

Knowledge is predominantly stored in organizations by means of individuals working in process teams. Given the increasing volume of existing knowledge in all areas, knowledge holders are pushed into specialization, that is, they focus on a specific body of knowledge. This leads to knowledge fragmentation in organizations, which in turn has been attacked by organizational learning advocates as a key reason for low process productivity and quality. Many organizational learning proponents, thus, have focused their efforts on finding ways to stimulate inter-functional knowledge sharing.

A relatively new and unorthodox approach to promote inter-functional knowledge sharing is to have workers participate in process improvement groups. While this has been hinted by early contributors of the organizational learning and total quality management movements, there was virtually no empirical evidence pointing to process improvement as an knowledge sharing catalyst.

This chapter discusses evidence that suggests that the number of knowledge-bearing communication exchanges in improvement processes is much higher than that observed in routine processes. It also shows that the proportion of knowledge content in communication exchanges in improvement processes is approximately 35 percent, compared with approximately 15 percent for routine processes. These findings are particularly significant because process improvement, unlike traditional knowledge transfer activities such as training sessions and committee meetings, has other numerous side effects that are obviously beneficial. Perhaps the most important among them is process improvement itself.

Endnotes

[1] This statement is often attributed to John Kenneth Galbraith. Born in 1908 in Iona State, Ontario, Galbraith is an internationally acclaimed economist and scholar whose seminal theoretical work has been influential in several areas of organizational research, including the incipient field of Information Systems. Given the scope and importance of his theoretical contributions, many question why he never received a Nobel Prize.

[2] In the same way as the terms metalanguage and metadata are used to refer,

respectively, to a higher-level language used to talk about other languages, and to higher-level data about other data sets.

[3] Novell Groupwise is a leading commercial groupware product distributed by Novell Corporation.

[4] Note that the last statement is a generic statement that expresses a generalization— "something will always happen at a given time of the year". Although this type of statement may be seen as *knowledge*, because it allows for prediction of the future (however, this is done independently of information about the present), it is inconsistent with my operational definition of knowledge discussed in Chapter 3. Since in research it is good practice to stick with operational definitions, statements such as this are not counted as knowledge in my analysis. However, as I will show later in this chapter, this consideration had no effect on the main findings of the analysis.

Part II
Distributed Improvement
and Learning

Chapter 5

The Effects of Collaborative Technologies

Why *distributed* improvement and learning?

The information era is characterized by a tremendous explosion in the amount of information flowing within and outside organizations. Information flows internally between organizational functions (or organizational *roles*, usually distinguished by different job titles). Information flows outside the organizations when communication takes place between the organization and one of its suppliers or customers.

As discussed in previous chapters, one of the main reasons why such explosion of information flow is taking place is the specialization of knowledge. As more and more knowledge is produced on a global scale, the scope of knowledge that is possessed by individuals becomes increasing narrower. Individuals strive to hold in-depth knowledge in a very limited number of fields and subjects, or, in other words, they specialize. Specialization is an involuntary phenomenon, and follows from human cognitive and, most importantly, *time* limitations. In the information era, those who do not specialize tend to become less competitive, because they do not have the time to acquire the knowledge and skills needed to compete with others in specific fields of knowledge. If you do not believe me, try to think of anyone who could be a top criminal lawyer and, at the same time, an internationally renowned brain surgeon. Even if we are talking about a super-genius here, time constraints will prevent this from happening, as both specialties require years and years of study and focused practice.

However, as the number of different knowledge specialties increases, so does the need for organizations to hire and manage groups of experts who specialize in different subject areas. A typical mid-sized financial services firm, for example, has to maintain hundreds of experts who specialize in different areas of financial analysis. Each of these areas, e.g. mutual fund management and securities analysis, are themselves made up of dozens of experts who specialize in different economic sectors and industries, e.g. Asian government bonds and domestic high-tech stocks. The existence of such knowledge variety leads organizations into a high degree of departmentalization (Hunt, 1996), or the organization around a heterogeneous structure of work teams (Eason, 1996), to cope with the management complexity that it generates.

Previous studies have shown that a high degree of knowledge specialization and the resulting high degree of departmentalization correlate with an intense flow of information. My own research on this topic suggests the existence of a very strong correlation between the number of functions in a process and the number of information exchanges in it[1]. That is, the trend towards knowledge specialization seen today is also leading to a severe increase in the amount of information that has to be transferred in organizations.

To complicate the picture painted above, previous research has also pointed to a high correlation between knowledge and information flow[2]. That is, as the flow of information increases, so does the flow of knowledge. In fact, this seems to be caused by another interesting cognitive phenomenon. There appears to be an information exchange threshold above which knowledge *needs* to be exchanged as well. The existence of such threshold can be intuitively understood through the observation of the communication that takes place between pairs of workers engaged in a common process. For example, let us consider two people engaged in the process of developing a new toothbrush, each of them being an expert in their own field (e.g. plastic materials resistance and oral preventive medicine). In the beginning of their interaction, these two people exchange descriptive information so each can reach their own conclusions about their plans for new toothbrush features. However, at a

---

John and Mark are working on the development of a new toothbrush. In order to do so they have to exchange information *and* knowledge. The dialogue below illustrates an initial exchange of information (two first paragraphs) that leads to the need for an ensuing exchange of knowledge (last paragraph).

"John, you told me that the elasticity of the middle section of our toothbrushes will decrease next year. Why is that?"

"Mark, you're always the last to know things around here, aren't you? It is because we will be using high density polyethylene to manufacture them, instead of the softer low density polyethylene that we use today."

"What? John, can you explain this to me please."

"Well, high density polyethylene is a very strong and hard type of plastic. If we use this type of plastic in our toothbrushes, their middle sections will be much less elastic than they are now."

Figure 5.1: Information exchanges often lead to knowledge exchanges

certain point, they will start transferring information that does not make absolute sense to each other — i.e. information that cannot be processed based on the existing body of knowledge that each of these experts possesses. At this point they will have to start exchanging knowledge (see Figure 5.1).

The need for transferring increasing amounts of information and knowledge in organizations has been compounded by (or combined with) another set of trends.

Firstly, no longer do organizations need to rely on endowment factors (e.g. natural resources, cheap labor) to compete globally. Competitive advantage is now defined by the ability of organizations to acquire and deploy process-related knowledge (Porter, 1980; 1985). A good example of this is provided by Japanese automakers like Toyota and Mazda, which managed to successfully compete on the global market in spite of Japan's lack of natural resources and of a relatively expensive labor force. Just compare the success of Japan with that of other countries, like Brazil, for example, whose natural resources relevant to the automobile manufacturing industry have always been much more abundant and whose labor force has always been cheaper. It can clearly be seen that global industrial success has very little to do with country endowment factors.

Secondly, process-related knowledge is increasingly found in a geographically dispersed way. People with expertise in processes like pharmaceuticals research for example, can be found in places as far apart as California, Oregon, Pennsylvania, New Zealand, and Uruguay.

Thirdly, the capitalist principles of free market and competition have been increasingly finding widespread adoption around the world, particularly since the early 1990s. This has intensified competition among organizations in the same industry at a global level.

A sub-product of the above trends has been that organizations are increasingly moving towards what some refer to as the "virtual organization" paradigm (Davidow and Malone 1992; Mowshowitz, 1997). Virtual organizations produce and deliver their products independently of their physical location and structure. Their most important assets are not material, tangible assets, but knowledge assets. Many knowledge-intensive processes rely largely on the transfer of information and knowledge, which can be done through the transfer of data. And, more and more today, data transfer relies heavily on computer networks.

It should come as no surprise, then, that the higher the *degree of virtuality* of an organization, the more likely it is that it will rely on computer networks to support communication among its members. Local and wide area computer networks have the potential to support the acquisition, transfer, storage and use of geographically dispersed process-related knowledge and information.

However, as with more traditional organizations, process teams in virtual organizations also have to cope with process inefficiencies, and the need to share process-related knowledge. And given the distributed nature of such process teams, it becomes increasingly important that process improvement (PI) and organizational learning in virtual organizations be conducted in a distributed, asynchronous (i.e. time-disconnected) manner. Hence the importance of understanding the effects of asynchronous group support technologies on PI groups. After all, PI groups, as I have shown in Chapter 4, can be a powerful tool to achieve both process improvement and organizational learning.

In Chapter 4, I discussed the link between process improvement and organizational learning based on the analysis of a number of PI groups conducted at two New Zealand organizations, namely Waikato University and MAF Quality Management. In this chapter, I will discuss the effects of a type of asynchronous group support technology on these PI groups. As it was previously mentioned in Chapter 4, the technology used to support group communication was e-mail conferencing. The e-mail conferencing system allowed members to send e-mail messages to a central mailbox, which then automatically distributed the messages to all the other members of the group (e.g. as in Internet e-mail lists, or "Listservs"). Most groups had members who were physically dispersed, either in different offices of the same building or campus, or across different cities or campuses. Most group members belonged to the same process team, that is, they were involved in the execution of the same (typically interdepartmental) process, even though they were usually not co-located.

To facilitate understanding, I split technology effects into three main categories in this chapter. The first category of effects are those on the efficiency of PI groups, that is, on the organizational cost of PI groups and on the total number of simultaneous PI groups that an organization can possibly have at any given time. The second category of effects refers to the impact on the quality of the outcomes generated by the PI groups, i.e. on the quality of process improvement proposals. The third category relates to the effects on learning effectiveness, as perceived by PI group members. Each of these categories of effects is individually discussed next.

Efficiency effects from a group perspective

John Grinder[3] was the national manager of the training and certification arm of MAF Quality Management. He was responsible for ensuring that field inspectors had the training and the certification credentials to do their job, as required by government regulations. As MAF Quality Management had many offices spread throughout New Zealand, John had to rely on local centers to handle training and certification sessions. Such sessions involved government-accredited consulting and training firms, as well as international certification bodies, and MAF Quality Management's field inspectors. Many of these inspectors routinely audited the operations of meat and milk farms, packaged food manufacturers, and livestock enhancement companies, among other food-related organizations.

Spreadsheet-based applications had been developed independently by each local training and certification center to keep track of information about field inspectors and the suppliers of training and certification services. However, due to recent changes in government regulations, John needed to generate periodic reports of the status of training and certification of inspectors nationwide. Moreover, John believed these services could be partially delivered online to MAF Quality Management, through the use of computer networks. John believed that this could potentially improve the quality of training, by allowing full-time access to training material by instructors, and at the same time reduce its cost to MAF Quality Management. John wanted to improve the process he managed.

John could simply hire a team of consultants to redesign the whole process and develop a distributed computer system to integrate data from the several local centers scattered throughout the country. But John knew better than that. If he wanted the new process to work, John knew that he would have to explain to the local centers why it was necessary to change the way training and certification was carried out up until then. He also knew that he would have to give them the opportunity to propose process changes themselves. It was either this, or the local centers would resist any change. "*People don't dislike change,*" John said to himself. "*People dislike change being imposed on them.*"

The problem was that, in order to get everyone's input regarding the process change, John would have to bring together a group of at least 20 people, representing each of the various local centers. And he was not sure his quarterly budget would allow him to pay for the travel and accommodation expenses of all these people. Not to mention buyout fees that some offices wanted to charge him to compensate for the hours the staff would spend in the process redesign— MAF Quality Management's administrative structure was highly decentralized, with many departments independently handling their own budgets. He decided to run the whole discussion as a PI group whose members would interact through an e-mail conferencing system. He contacted each of the local centers by phone, and invited 23 people to participate in the e-mail-supported PI group.

The discussion lasted about three months, and the whole group met face-to-face only once at the end of the discussion. John estimates that the use of the e-mail conferencing system has saved him over $60,000 only in travel and accommodation expenses. Also, he did not have to pay for the staff-hours spent in the electronic discussion, as staff did not have to physically leave their offices during the discussion. Moreover, he was pleased with the results. Representatives of local centers proposed and, after some discussion, almost unanimously agreed on adopting a new set of procedures. They went some way towards specifying software and hardware requirements for a computer system to enable the new procedures, which was soon after implemented by a software firm.

The organizational cost of improvement groups is reduced

Although the picture painted above may seem a bit too rosy, it is true to the general trend observed in the PI groups I have facilitated and studied (see Appendix B). However, an analysis of the PI group descriptions in Appendix B shows that not all groups were as successful as the group led by John. Some of the groups studied, for example, failed to reach a consensus about process changes, and as a result no changes were either proposed or implemented by these groups. A nutshell discussion of PI group success factors, based on the analysis of the 12 groups described in Appendix B, is provided in Chapter 6. Some considerations on the general quality of computer-supported PI group outcomes are made later in this chapter.

Nevertheless, an important trend that was observed in the twelve computer-supported PI groups conducted at Waikato University and MAF Quality Management is their reduced cost compared with similar face-to-face PI groups. Group members themselves indicated such cost reduction, in interviews. They were asked to compare the computer-supported PI groups with previous face-to-face PI groups in which they had participated.

Twenty-nine out of 46 PI group members at Waikato University, or 63 percent, spontaneously remarked that computer support had reduced the costs of member participation in PI groups. Two main reasons for this cost reduction were mentioned. A reduction in disruption costs, or costs related to staff having to interrupt their routine activities in order to participate in the PI groups, was the reason given by most of the interviewees. The other reason was a reduction in the time each member spent participating, either actively or passively, in the group discussion. When asked about a possible reduction in travel and accommodation costs, all PI group members stated that those cost reductions were very significant in most groups, but too obvious to be mentioned in the interviews. The quote below is from a faculty member who had been involved in a PI group dealing with legal issues related to the provision of academic advice to students:

It is very hard [...] to organize meetings around people's schedules. It was probably a lot quicker to respond to [electronic contributions] than to get together and sit in a face-to-face meeting and talk about other things for a while until you get on with the subject at hand. [...] It probably increased the input that you got from other departments.

At MAF Quality Management, structured interviews indicated that approximately 78 percent of the respondents viewed computer-supported PI groups as having cost much less to the organization than face-to-face PI groups. This is illustrated in Figure 5.2, where the distribution of response frequencies suggests a statistically strong trend[4] in the direction of a collective perception that computer support leads to a reduction in group cost.

At MAF Quality Management, the average time spent by a member of a PI group discussion was estimated at slightly over 20 hours if the discussions had been carried out exclusively through face-to-face meetings. This time was reduced by computer

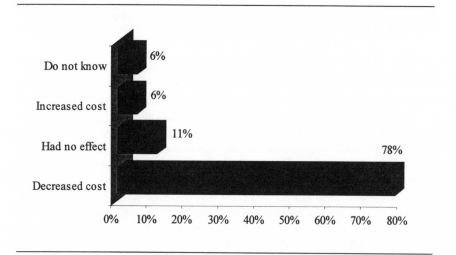

Figure 5.2: Perceptions about computer support impact on group cost

support to about one hour and 30 minutes, which was the average time spent by ordinary group members (i.e. all group members with the exception of the group leader). This amounts to an average reduction of approximately 93 percent. For group leaders, the average time spent in the group discussion went from twenty hours to approximately seven hours, according to direct time measurements. Although less than for ordinary members, this amounts to a 65 per cent reduction in the group leader participation time.

The bottom-line money saving per group was gauged through an absolute dollar amount estimate, which proved to be very attractive. To obtain such estimate I assumed, very conservatively, that a group member costs the organization on average 15 dollars per hour. As the average number of members in a PI group is nine (averaged based on the PI groups at MAF Quality Management), then computer support reduced the cost per group to the organization in at least $2,415. This is the price of a good desktop computer with basic office automation software installed in it. Note that group facilitation (provided by a PI consultant, for example) and travel expense savings have been disregarded in the calculation of this figure.

The lifetime of improvement groups is reduced

Another trend observed in the computer-supported PI groups conducted at Waikato University and MAF Quality Management was an apparently shortened lifetime, in comparison with face-to-face PI groups. And yet, as it will be seen later in this chapter, this reduced lifetime has not led to a decrease in the quality of group outcomes (i.e. the process redesign proposals generated by the groups). PI group lifetime was measured in days, from the inception of the group to its formal cessation.

The lifetime of the PI groups conducted at Waikato University varied from thirty-two to fifty-four days, with an average of about 40 days, and a standard deviation of approximately nine days. At MAF Quality Management, PI group lifetime was slightly shorter. It ranged from ten to 29 days, averaging at 22 days,

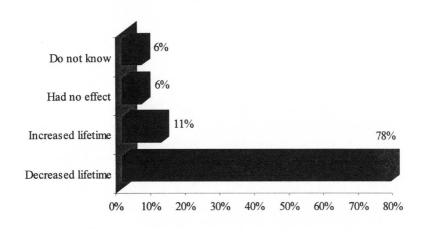

Figure 5.3: Perceptions about computer support impact on group lifetime

with a standard deviation of approximately eight days.

At Waikato University, many PI group members voluntarily and consistently noted a perceived decrease of group lifetime as a consequence of computer support, though no frequency distribution analysis was performed. At MAF Quality Management, interviewees' responses displayed a strong trend towards the perception that computer-supported PI groups had been completed in less time, measured in number of days, than face-to-face PI groups. Approximately 78 percent of the interviewees were of this opinion, which indicates a statistically strong trend[5]. This is illustrated in Figure 5.3, which, coincidentally, is similar to Figure 5.2.

The main cause for the reduction of group lifetime, according to group members, had been a reduction in what many referred to as "group set up time." This was generally described as the time needed to accomplish group set up activities, such as defining a list of problems (or improvement opportunities) to be discussed by the group, selecting group members, and inviting those members to take part in the group. Many interviewees noted that while the time needed to carry out some of these activities had been curtailed by computer support, the need for other activities more typical of face-to-face meetings had been completely eliminated. Examples of such activities are choosing and preparing a venue for the group meetings, and coordinating member attendance.

Improvement initiatives are decentralized

Managers have long dominated the scene when it comes to changing their organizations. Total quality management tried to turn this picture around a little, by showing that the best prepared to improve processes were those who carried them out, not those who managed them. Yet, in spite of this, process improvement has long suffered from an over-reliance on managers. And the business process re-engineering movement, with its top-down change philosophy, somewhat legitimized this situation.

However, managers are just a few when compared with the body of line staff in organizations. And with the current corporate downsizing trend, the manager-to-employee ratio is being steadily reduced, day after day. One management "guru" has been quoted as proudly saying that, "where years ago there was one manager for each seven employees, now there is one for each 100 employees." Obviously, this is an achievement for many organizations, particularly those where management levels are more of an information buffer than anything else. After all, managers, like other support and control entities, do not usually add value to customers.

But as managers grow more and more scarce, they also become busier. Their endless stream of business meetings and improvised interactions (Kurke and Aldrich, 1983; Mintzberg, 1975) becomes more fragmented, and the likelihood that they will want, or have the time to participate in more meetings grows increasingly slim. Such environment, though purportedly more cost-effective in terms of management expenses and utilization, is not a fertile ground for process improvement ventures. Managers, whose leadership and seniority are needed to legitimize and give weight to improvement efforts, are hardly available.

Apparently, computer support reverses the picture above, by reducing the demand for senior leadership in PI groups. At Waikato University, some PI group leaders spontaneously remarked that computer support had made it considerably easier for them to lead their PI groups. None of these leaders were the most senior members of their PI groups. One of these group leaders, who was the most junior person in his group, stated that:

> [...] leading a face-to-face meeting [with the same group members] would be considerably more demanding and stressful for me.

His junior status in the organization was perceived by the leader as likely to have considerably hindered him from leading the PI group, had the group been conducted only through face-to-face discussions.

At both Waikato University and MAF Quality Management, similar reasons were put forth by PI group members for the reduction of in-group demand for leadership seniority apparently associated with computer support. The most common reasons were:

- A suppression of social cues by the electronic medium, which could differentiate junior from senior members;
- A reduction in the influence that individual members have on the group, which was seen as likely to increase with seniority in face-to-face groups; and
- A suppression of hierarchy barriers to an open discussion.

Note that these reasons almost imply a sense of partial anonymity in computer-mediated discussions. Yet, none of the PI groups involved anonymous electronic contributions at all. The following quote from a group leader illustrates the member perceptions underlying their explanations:

> Normally if I am in a [face-to-face] situation and with [another member's name - removed], who is my boss, his opinion counts over mine, when I'm sitting in the same room ... on e-mail I feel just as equal—I don't feel that he will influence me or that his opinion will be more important than mine. Because I feel like I can just freely put my ideas on an e-mail and I don't feel threatened by him being above me. You [referring to PI group members in general] are all equals on e-mail ... I definitely don't think about the hierarchy structure when I'm on e-mail, but I do think about it when I'm sitting in a room and I see [names of two other group members - removed] sitting there. And they get a lot more influential because of that, because everybody is a bit more wary of what they say, whereas on e-mail people are more likely to say what they've got to say.

Figure 5.4 shows statistically significant (according to Chi-square tests) perception trends for members polled across different PI groups that provide majority support for all of these reasons.

The number of possible improvement groups is increased

As demand for senior leadership is reduced by computer support, so does the need to rely on managers to lead PI groups. Ordinary PI group members, as opposed to leaders, do not need to be managers either; they can be anyone within the organization or even come from outside. They can be external customers and

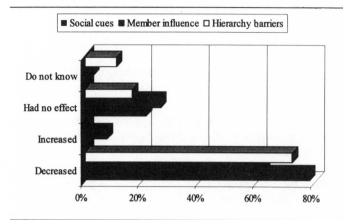

Figure 5.4: Computer support impact on factors influencing group demand for senior leadership

suppliers, for example. A direct and obvious consequence of this relaxation in leadership requirements afforded by technology is an increase in the number of possible PI groups that can be run at a given time in the organization. To this, it can be added that the lifetime of PI groups is reduced by computer support, making this effect even stronger. That is, the increase in organizational PI groups capacity is combined with a shorter lifetime to yield a potential expansion in the number of PI groups that can be conducted per unit of time (e.g. per quarter).

This combined effect could be clearly observed at Waikato University. This organization had instituted "official PI days" in which staff and faculty members were expected to engage full-time in PI group discussions during a whole day. PI groups would look into current business processes and related organizational procedures and regulations, and then propose changes aimed at process improvement. Although these group efforts were typically seen as relatively successful by most, their frequency was very low, usually twice every year. As soon as computer support was made available to staff and faculty, five groups were conducted within less than a quarter.

Many PI group members at both Waikato University and MAF Quality Management pointed out that computer support had made it much easier for them to start and conduct their PI discussions with a minimum of disruption for them and their fellow group members. Several of these members spontaneously mentioned a reduction of group set up time as an explanation for their perceptions.

Effects on group outcome quality

Whatever efficiency gains are obtained through computer support, it would be difficult to justify the use of computer support if it impaired the quality of group outcomes. The main outcome of any PI group is the process change proposal generated by the group. Such outcome is the focus of this section. Here, we are concerned with the impact that computer support has on the quality of process

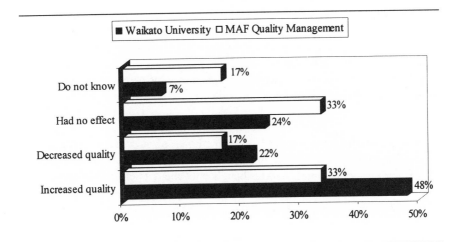

Figure 5.5: Perceptions of computer support impact on process redesign quality

improvement proposals in comparison with that of face-of-face groups.

PI group members were asked to compare their experience in the computer-supported PI group discussion, with that of similar face-to-face situations. An aggregate analysis of their answers indicates an interesting, yet slight trend towards a perceived increase in the quality of process redesign proposals generated by groups. This trend was observed at both Waikato University and MAF Quality Management, and was marginally stronger at the education institution. Figure 5.5 shows the frequency distribution of answers from PI group members regarding process redesign quality in both organizations.

As in previous analyses of perception frequency distributions, I used a statistical analysis technique called Chi-square test of independence to establish the statistical strength of the perception trend. This test revealed a five-percent probability that the trend observed at Waikato University was due to chance; for MAF Quality Management, the test yielded 63 percent of certainty regarding the perception trend, or a 37 percent probability that the trend was due to chance. In other words, if I was to generalize the findings to other areas (or departments) of either organization, I would be much more confident the validity of such generalization for Waikato University, than for MAF Quality Management.

A decisive trend towards an increase in group outcome quality due to computer support cannot be inferred based on the evidence collected, as there was a considerable number of members who perceived it otherwise. Seventeen percent of the PI group members at MAF Quality Management, and 22 percent at Waikato University, perceived a decrease in quality due to computer support (see Figure 5.5). Nevertheless, the perception frequency distribution in Figure 5.5 does suggest a general and statistically strong trend towards a *non-negative* effect on process redesign quality. Seventy-two percent of the respondents at Waikato University perceived either an increase or a null effect in process redesign quality; this proportion was about 66 percent at MAF Quality Management.

Most of the group members who perceived an increase in quality explained it by an improvement in the quality of individual contributions from PI group members interacting through the computer system. That is, they noticed an increase in the quality of individual contributions, which, they reasoned, had led to an increase in the quality of the process redesign proposals generated by their groups. The remarks below, from a PI group member, provide a good illustration of this general perception:

> You think more when you're writing something, so you produce a better quality contribution. Take for example what [member's name - removed] wrote, she wrote a lot and it seemed that she thought a lot about it before she e-mailed it to the group. She wasn't just babbling off the top of her head, she tended to think out what she was writing. I know I did it a lot, specially my first message. I really thought a lot to put it together.

The majority of those who perceived a decrease in process redesign quality believed that it had been caused by inherent characteristics of computer-mediated communication. In these members' judgment, interacting through the computer system increased the ambiguity in the PI group discussion. This was particularly true, according to these PI group members, in the analysis stage of a PI group, where the group analyzes the target process (or processes) for redesign. Group members had to build a shared understanding of the process being analyzed in this stage, so they could later effectively contribute process change suggestions.

Most groups had a multi-departmental composition. Which meant that differences in the technical language used by different members had often become obstacles that had to be removed if the discussion was to proceed successfully. The asynchronous and distributed nature of the computer-supported communication in the PI groups prevented immediate feedback and the use of non-verbal cues (e.g. gestures), which apparently made it more difficult, in the opinion of some members, to remove obstacles to a shared understanding about the process being analyzed.

Still, the percentage of respondents who were of the opinion that redesign quality had been decreased by the use of group technology was comparatively low. This indicates that the higher quality observed in individual contributions might have offset the communication constraints inherent in the electronic medium. As a consequence, a neutral, bending towards positive, overall effect on process redesign quality can be inferred from the evidence collected.

Effects on organizational learning effectiveness

In Chapter 4, I concluded that process improvement itself fosters, as a group process, knowledge communication. This conclusion was largely based on content analysis of communication interactions between people carrying out process improvement and routine processes in real organizational settings. In this section our main concern is shifted to the effect that computer support has on the effectiveness of organizational learning. Even though, as shown in Chapter 4, more knowledge communication is apparently closely linked to the task of improving processes, it is important to establish whether *computer support* does not interfere negatively with the learning process that PI group members undergo when they exchange knowledge and information.

The perception aired by some PI group members that computer support may increase communication ambiguity, which was discussed in the previous section, is consistent with previous research, notably research associated with a very influential theory of media adoption and use known as Media Richness Theory (Daft and Lengel, 1986). Media Richness Theory argues that different communication media possess varied amounts of an abstract property called "richness", which relates to the capacity of the media to convey more or less information and knowledge. According to Media Richness Theory, the richest communication medium is that afforded by face-to-face interaction (Lee, 1994). Media that prevent non-verbal cues from being communicated and which delay feedback, like e-mail, are seen as less rich than media which allow immediate feedback and the communication of non-verbal cues; features that are found in abundance in face-to-face meetings (Daft et al., 1987; Lengel and Daft, 1988). It follows that asynchronous and distributed computer conferencing systems provide a leaner medium for communication than do face-to-face meetings. And, argues Media Richness Theory, lean media are less adequate to the transfer of knowledge and information[6] than rich media.

Given expectations based on Media Richness Theory, pessimistic forecasts about the impact of computer support on learning in PI groups can be reasonably expected. Moreover, the empirical research literature on asynchronous and distributed group support technologies has reported a number of failures of these technologies to support interdepartmental knowledge communication (Kock, 1997). Among other reasons, these failures have been explained by:

- The inherent ambiguity that the electronic medium adds to group communication (Rogers, 1992);
- Social norms and reward systems adopted by firms, that can themselves become obstacles to knowledge sharing (Orlikowski, 1992); and
- The lack of balance between the benefits to those who have to do extra work because of the introduction of a group support system and those who do not (Grudin, 1994).

The perceptions of the PI group members regarding individual learning, however, contradicted the gloomy picture painted by previous theories and empirical research. Group members were consistently positive in their views about computer support impact on individual learning, as shown in the distribution of perceptions depicted in Figure 5.6. As with previous analyses of frequency distribution, this trend was checked for statistical significance. This revealed that the probability that the trend observed was due to chance is about 2.5 percent for the frequency distribution at Waikato University and 0.5 percent for MAF Quality Management. That is, it can be safely assumed that the trends are not due to chance. My interpretation is that these trends are most likely a result of underlying capabilities of the technology to move group behavior towards learning-conducive situations.

A little unexpected is the explanatory direction pointed at by the evidence, particularly the evidence presented in the previous section. There, group members perceived an increase in the quality of their group outcomes (i.e. process redesign

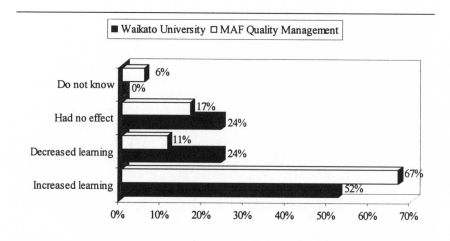

Figure 5.6: Perceptions about computer support impact on learning

proposals) as resulting from computer mediation. One of the main reasons for this, according to the group members themselves, was the better preparation of individual contributions by group members. Yet, the same members perceived computer mediation itself as having the potential to increase communication ambiguity. What is the direction at which this evidence points in light of the perception trends shown in this section? It appears the answer is that the leanness of the communication medium afforded by computer support has led to an adaptive behavior that over-came, at least partially, the constraints posed by the leaner medium. More knowledge was communicated (which is consistent with the conclusions reached at in Chapter 4), which led to higher perceived learning.

When asked to explain their answers regarding computer support impact on individual learning, there was a clear convergence in the answers given by PI group members. Most of the relatively small number of members who perceived a decrease in individual learning, suggested that this was due to a reduction in the degree of interaction caused by computer mediation. That is, less individual contributions are made in computer-mediated than in face-to-face discussions, and thus less learning takes place. The idea that computer mediation leads to reduced group interaction is certainly incorrect for same-time-same-place computer interaction, where the num-ber of contributions per unit of time has consistently been found to have been increased (Dennis et al., 1996, Sheffield and Gallupe, 1993). However, in my study of asynchronous (time-disconnected) and distributed computer-supported groups, partially discussed here, group interaction indeed seemed to have been considerably reduced by computer mediation. Yet, whether this led to reduced information and knowledge exchange is doubtful, since the length of individual contributions and their knowledge content appears to have been considerably increased. This effect may be partly due to computer mediation.

At MAF Quality Management, the two main reasons presented for the perceived increase in individual learning were better quality of and more sincere individual contributions. PI group members linked the increase in sincerity to a sense of personal insulation fostered by the computer mediation. That is, often when members interact via a computer they feel less inhibited to freely express their feelings and ideas. This perception is partially supported by previous studies of e-mail communication in organizational contexts (Sproull and Kiesler, 1986), distributed and anonymous groups (Jessup and Tansik, 1991), and groups composed of introverts and extroverts (Yellen et al., 1995). PI group members at Waikato University gave the same explanations. Yet, they added a new one to our repertoire, which was that member learning was improved by the higher departmental heterogeneity afforded by computer support. According to these members the distributed and time-independent nature of the computer-mediated interaction allowed for a larger number of departments to be represented in each PI group. This in turn brought into the discussion more ideas and individual perspectives that were new to many group members, thus leading to a perception of increased individual learning.

Summary and concluding remarks

The ever-growing amount of information flowing in organizations, knowledge specialization, and geographical distribution of expertise are among the main factors driving the expansion in the use of computers to support team-based processes. At the same time, these factors also lead to more and more processes being carried by distributed teams. This environment poses obstacles to traditional face-to-face interaction, which, combined with growing competitive forces, drives firms into increasingly using computers for process improvement and organizational learning.

This chapter presents and discusses solid evidence that points to an increase of process improvement group efficiency due to computer support. Efficiency gains are reflected in reduced group cost, lifetime, and reliance on managers. Additionally, the number of simultaneous process improvement groups is increased by computer support.

The evidence also points to increases in perceived group outcome quality and organizational learning effectiveness, as a result of computer support. These findings, combined with those regarding group efficiency, provide a sound basis for the endorsement of asynchronous collaborative technologies as tools for process improvement and organizational learning.

Endnotes

[1] The correlation coefficient found was .86, using the Pearson product-moment method, which suggests that 86 percent of the variation in the variable *information exchanges* can be explained through functional diversification. The likelihood that such high coefficient of correlation is due to chance was found to be lower than five percent (Kock et al., 1997).

[2] This correlation has been found to be as high as .75 *(Pearson)*. The likelihood that this high correlation is due to chance was found to be lower than five percent (Kock et al., 1997).

[3] As with the rest of this book, names and some situations in this chapter have been disguised to honor confidentiality agreements.

[4] The likelihood that the perception trend observed is due to chance is lower than one-tenth of a percent, as indicated by a statistical test called Chi-square test of independence between frequency distributions.

[5] The likelihood that the perception trend observed is due to chance is lower than one-tenth of a percent, as indicated by a Chi-square test of independence between frequency distributions.

[6] The theory actually claims that "uncertainty" and "equivocality" reduction are better accomplished through richer communication media. It is my interpretation that uncertainty is reduced through the exchange of information, and equivocality through the exchange of knowledge, according to the definitions of information and knowledge provided earlier in this book. Hence my statement regarding media richness and the communication of knowledge and information.

Chapter 6

Successful Distributed Improvement and Learning

The trend towards organizational improvement

The idea of process-focused improvement has been with us for many years. Many speculate that it is as old as the total quality management movement, which began in Japan in the 1950s. Some think the idea is much older, dating back to the time of the Pharaohs of Egypt. At least two popular management movements incorporated this idea. One of these management movements is the just mentioned total quality management, whose popularity reached a peak in the US in the 1980s, and whose main figure was William Deming. The other is business process re-engineering, which was developed and became very popular in 1990s, and whose main proponent was Michael Hammer.

Examples of process-focused improvement have been and still are found in abundance in the organizational world, whether the organizations considered are public or private, for profit or not. Therefore, there is plenty of organizational data that can be used to establish how successful process-focused improvement projects have been so far. Moreover, as the total quality management reached is peak of popularity in the 1980s, there is now long-term organizational evidence that allows for the analysis of total quality management projects over several years.

Choi and Behling (1997) have summarized studies of total quality management. This summary suggests some lackluster results. For example, a survey of 500 manufacturing and service firms in the US indicated that two-thirds of their executives believe that total quality management programs have not made them more competitive. Another survey of 100 British firms, where total quality management programs had been implemented, indicated that only one-fifth perceived their programs as having significantly impacted their firms' performance. Yet another survey conducted by the American Electronics Association suggested that the popularity of total quality management programs among its member firms had dropped from 86 percent in 1988 to only 73 percent in 1991. The same survey revealed that, in 63 percent of the firms, total quality management programs that had been in operation for an average of 2.5 years had reduced defects by no more than 10 percent. An evaluation of total quality management programs by McKinsey & Company found that two-thirds of them had been discontinued due to failing short of the original expectations.

On the other hand, Hendricks and Singhal (1997) conducted a study where quality-award-winning companies were compared against a sample of control firms. Their study spanned a period of ten years, comprising six years before and three years after the quality awards were conferred. One of their findings was that the mean change in the operating income for the award-winning firms was 107 percent higher than that of the control sample. Another finding was that the mean increase in sales had been 64 percent higher for the award-winning firms, which suggests firms that have won quality awards have done considerably better on sales growth than the control firms. On the other hand, only weak evidence was found that the award-winning firms had been more successful in controlling costs than the firms in the control sample.

The business process re-engineering history is somewhat different. It started with case studies showing the almost miraculous potential of the combination of a focus on organizational processes and a radical approach to change (Hammer, 1990; Hammer and Champy, 1993). Yet, not too long after these initial case studies were published, a survey of private firms in the US and Europe, conducted at the peak of the re-engineering movement by one of its forerunners (Champy, 1995), indicated a failure rate as high as 70 percent.

No doubt mixed findings exist regarding the success and failure of process improvement approaches and projects, whether they resemble total quality management, re-engineering or any other less known process-focused improvement approach. Yet, process improvement is still so widely practiced among organizations of all sizes that one could wonder whether its bad side is being ignored or there is nothing better around. A topic closely related to total quality management, ISO 9000 certification, is as popular as ever, particularly among exports-oriented companies and "satellite" part suppliers of large manufacturers (Kock and McQueen, 1997; Ruddell and Stevens, 1998). Information technology companies that built and marketed products around the process re-engineering idea, such as Germany's software giant SAP, have done, in the period between the start of the re-engineering movement and 1997, as well as any company in their industry could. SAP reported a record 1.67 billion marks ($929.9 million) in pretax profit in 1997, compared with 967 million marks in 1996. SAP's sales in 1997 were 6.02 billion marks, up 62% and also a record (Rose, 1998).

My conclusion is that although different measures of success will yield different, and often conflicting, results, the trend towards organizational process improvement will remain strong for at least one or two more decades. After the barrage of criticism of process-based improvement methods by business specialists and company strategy commentators in the mid-1990s, many management experts seem now to acknowledge this inevitable trend. Moreover, many information technology experts working in "hot" new areas also seem to hold similar views, which they air as often as they can. Umar (1997, p. 4), in the introductory chapter of his book on client/server environments, summarizes the organizational demands and circumstances surrounding and sustaining the trend towards process-focused improvement:

> Enterprises in the 1990s and beyond are typically characterized by flatter organizational structures, increased demands for flexibility, pressures to respond quickly to market conditions, intense local and global competition, and continued business-process reengineering and improvements for enterprise efficiency.

Among other things, developments in information technology will both support and feed this trend. Information technology is not only a tool that enables organizations to deal with change by supporting the implementation of new business processes. It also creates competitive disparities among organizations that feed the pressure for change and, as a result, the need for process improvement.

Finally, we cannot forget that process improvement builds on a well-established foundation of techniques for systems analysis and design, whose popularity increases as the use of information technology in organizations grows. Why such increase in popularity? One of the reasons is because these techniques are fundamental for new process implementation and task automation. I do not see any signs of a possible a reduction in the use of computers and computer applications in organizations in the near future. On the contrary, an accelerated growth is the most likely prospect.

The trend towards organizational learning

One of the key ideas behind "organizational learning" is that organizations, as collective entities, acquire, store and use knowledge over time. And, it is now widely accepted that a firm's competitive advantage depends heavily on its ability to acquire, store and use unique knowledge in a way that allows the firm to produce and deliver "products" that have a singular appeal to its customers (Spender, 1996; Prahalad and Hamel, 1990).

But has not this notion been commonplace for a long time? Have not many people known for years that knowledge management and organizational competitiveness are closely related? I believe the answer is "yes". Nevertheless, we have seen since the mid-1990s a widespread and growing interest in organizational learning, with an intensity that has not been seen before. Why is that so? Is it because organizational learning is a new fad? Certainly not, as the concept has been discussed at least since the 1970s by people such as Harvard professor Chris Argyris and others.

The key to explain the present interest in organizational learning lies, in my opinion, in two factors. One, which is eminently socioeconomic, is the accelerated growth of the current operational body of knowledge that is relevant to the creation of goods and services (as well as other organizational outputs such as software and information). The other factor is closely related to how the human species evolved, from a biological perspective, namely the current human cognitive limitations. Let me explain the nature of these factors and how they affect our interest in management approaches such as organizational learning.

Speculations about the speed with which the available body of knowledge grows vary widely. Some believe that it doubles every two years, while others speculate that it triples every eighteen months. Measures of knowledge also vary widely, from number of registered patents to number of articles published in academic journals. Given this, and until we have a widely accepted knowledge measurement unit, it is meaningless to try to precisely estimate how much knowledge is created per year. Yet, at least two things are obvious. First, the amount of knowledge created in any generic field of research every two years is *very large*; certainly larger than what an average person would be able to absorb without specialization —i.e. without a focus on specific knowledge within one (or a few) field(s). For example, the amount of knowledge in the field of distributed computing, which practically did not exist in the 1950s, had grown so large by the 1990s that it spun off a number of sub-fields, such as that of client-server computing. Second, the speed with which knowledge is created has been increasing. In other words, much less knowledge, however it is measured, was created per year in the 1950s than in the 1990s.

I pointed out above that people specialize in sub-fields, often creating a number of them in the process, because they cannot assimilate the growing body of knowledge being created in higher-level fields. That is, specialization is a function of knowledge growth and cognitive limitations. And, specialization leads to knowledge fragmentation or, in other words, the creation of new sub-fields of knowledge. Where does the growing interest in organizational learning fits in this picture? Well, knowledge fragmentation leads to functional fragmentation in organizations. For example, John is the new "web-site administrator", an organizational function (or role, or job description) which entails a well-defined set of responsibilities, which in turn require specialized knowledge. This function did not exist in the 1980s, because the world-wide web became popular only in the 1990s.

The problem is that John, the web-site administrator, must hold a considerable body of knowledge, and keep up with the new knowledge being created by the day (if not the hour) in his area, the area of web-site administration. Hence, John cannot combine this organizational function with other related functions, such as the more established function of network administrator. Network administration has then to be done by another person, say, Karen. This is a clear example of functional fragmentation that occurred late in the 1990s. The "old" role of network administrator has now spawned at least one related role, web site administrator, due to the creation of new knowledge about web-site technology. The problem is that John and Karen are still going to be involved in a few common organizational processes, like the one of providing computer support to internal customers who need network access rights to set up their own web pages. As such, John and Karen need to share "some" knowledge. And, here is where organizational learning comes in, as inter-functional knowledge sharing is one of the most important aspects of organizational learning (Redding and Catalanello, 1994).

The trend towards virtual organizations

As discussed above, there is a noticeable trends towards process improvement and organizational learning; trends that are unlikely to fade away soon. This is because both process improvement and organizational learning allow organizations to face problems that are typical of highly competitive and knowledge intensive economies. In the years to come, the terms used for process improvement and organizational learning may change, but the focus on process-based change and knowledge acquisition and deployment will continue.

Yet, a third major trend must be discussed; a technological trend. Since the mid-1980s, there has been an accelerated increase in the use of computer networks to provide communication links within and between organizations. Electronic communication links within organizations have been established through local area networks (LANs) and, more recently, "intranets". Similar links between organizations have been established through wide area networks (WANs) and, more recently, the Internet and inter-organizational computer systems all over the world.

As discussed in Chapter 5, an accelerated increase in the number of knowledge specializations and their globalization has accompanied this worldwide diffusion of computer networks, which have made it possible for a number of organizations to become independent of geographical constraints. This had, in turn, led a number of organizations to structure themselves around communication networks. These organizations also moved towards organizational paradigms that place emphasis on flexibility, knowledge accumulation and deployment, and distributed teamwork. One such paradigm is that of the "virtual organization" (Davidow and Malone, 1992; Mowshowitz, 1997).

The concept of virtual organizations has become one of the "hottest" management topics of the 1990s, particularly given the possibilities afforded by local and wide area networks of computers. Advantages of moving from physically aggregated organizational units towards electronically linked ones have been widely publicized. Facilities rental and maintenance costs can be considerably reduced or eliminated. Employees can work from their own homes or from distributed offices near their houses. Company offices can spread over large geographical areas, reaching a larger number of customers than physically aggregated offices would. And, operations data can still be monitored in a centralized manner. Clients can purchase goods, services, and information irrespective of where they are in the world, without the need to travel long distances.

Given the three trends discussed above, it is reasonable to expect that there will be increasing pressure on organizations to find ways to carry out process improvement and organizational learning in a distributed, computer-mediated fashion. As more and more people interact through computers, the alternative to face competitive pressures and knowledge explosion will be to conduct thousands of face-to-face meetings. Unless we find out how to beam people around (like in Star Trek) at a very low cost, this is unlikely to be a feasible alternative. Perhaps it is time to try to understand what makes distributed process improvement and learning succeed.

Success factors: An analysis of twelve groups

In Chapters 4, I discussed the link between process improvement and organizational learning. In Chapter 5, I discussed the impact of collaborative technologies on process improvement and organizational learning. Now I will complement those discussions with an investigation on what makes distributed process improvement groups succeed with the support of collaborative technologies. As in Chapter 5, process improvement (PI) groups conducted at two New Zealand organizations,

Waikato University and MAF Quality Management are analyzed here.

As with much of the evidence presented in this book, the evidence discussed in this chapter is a refinement of previous analyses conducted, and whose preliminary results appeared in conference proceedings and journal articles. Such previous analyses helped unveil patterns for future study. In the case of success factors, previous analyses led me to pay particular attention to three types of factors:

- Leadership factors, which relate to characteristics of the leaders (or moderators) of computer-supported process improvement groups;
- Membership factors, which relate to group membership; and
- "Group" factors, which relate to general characteristics of each group, including characteristics of the target process.

In my analyses of interviews conducted with group members and other individuals (most of whom interacted with group members) I tried to summarize perception patterns related to group success. This summarization led to the building of three main tables, where each factor was split into a few sub-factors (or variables). These variables were then assigned qualitative values along a three-point scale: low, medium, and high. The results were matched against the content of the dependent variable *group success* for each factor separately. The three following sections discuss the findings that emerged from those analyses.

Leadership factors

Table 6.1 shows the variation of leader-related variables along the twelve groups, together with the degree of success obtained by each group. Groups are ordered on the table based on their degree of success, the most successful at the top and the least successful at the bottom. From left to right, the three first columns of Table 6.1 show: a brief description of each process[1] targeted for redesign, the organization to which each process belongs, and the degree of success obtained by each group. The three last columns on Table 6.1 show the leader's relative status among all group members, the leader's degree of attempted control of the group discussion, and the degree of involvement of the leader in the process being targeted for redesign.

It can be inferred from Table 6.1 that, when taken individually, neither the leader's relative status or attempted control consistently affected group success. On the other hand, the process involvement of the group leader was consistently related with a high degree of group success. With the exception of the group whose target was the process of *staff training and development* at MAF Quality Management, leaders who owned the processes targeted by the groups were able to lead their groups through to a successful completion. There were also two examples in which the leader was a key process member of highly successful groups, but no instance where the leader's process involvement was low and still the group succeeded.

"Owning" a process, here, means to be the principal coordinator of the several activities making up the process, or the one who is the main responsible for process throughput. It is likely that a person in a management position will own at least one process, but this may not always be the case.

Process description	Organization	Success	Relative status	Leader's	
				Attempted control	Process involvement
Newsletter editing	MAF	High: Group agreed on process changes, from which all were implemented with positive results	High: Senior manager	Low: Asked and individually thanked members for opinions, let the discussion flow	High: Process owner
University course	Waikato	High: Group agreed on process changes, from which all were implemented with positive results	Low: Part-time graduate assistant	Low: Asked for opinions and let the discussion flow	High: Process owner
Student assignment handling	Waikato	High: Group agreed on process changes, from which all were implemented with positive results	Medium: Division manager	Low: Asked and individually thanked members for opinions, let the discussion flow	High: Process owner
International graduate student support	Waikato	High: Group agreed on process changes, from which all were partially or fully implemented with positive results	Medium: Division manager	High: Half-way through the discussion, unilaterally changed its topic	High: Process owner
International student adaptation support	Waikato	High: Group agreed on process changes, from which all were partially of fully implemented with positive results	Medium: Middle manager	Low: Asked and individually thanked members for opinions, let the discussion flow	High: Process owner
IT users support	MAF	High: Group agreed on process changes, from which three quarters were implemented with positive results	Medium: Senior computer support person	Medium: Tried to keep group discussion on focus	Medium: Key process member
Software support	MAF	High: Group agreed on process changes, from which two thirds were implemented with positive results	Medium: Middle manager	Low: Asked for opinions and let the discussion flow	High: Process owner
Pest/disease outbreak communication	MAF	High: Group agreed on process changes, from which one third were implemented with positive results	High: Senior manager	Low: Asked and individually thanked members for opinions, let the discussion flow	Medium: Key process member
Undergraduate academic support	Waikato	Medium: Group agreed on process changes, from which none was implemented	Medium: Senior liaison person	Low: Asked for opinions and let the discussion flow	Low: Marginally involved in the process
Quality management consulting	MAF	Low: No agreement on process changes was achieved	Low: Middle manager (amid several senior managers)	Low: Asked and individually thanked members for opinions, let the discussion flow	Medium: Provided process-related training
Staff training and development	MAF	Low: Unfocused discussion, the group was discontinued without agreeing on any process changes	High: Senior manager	High: Tried to obtain specific information from members based on individual assumptions	High: Process owner
Student computer support	Waikato	Low: No agreement on process changes was achieved	Low: Part-time graduate assistant	Medium: Pointed out digressions, tried to keep group discussion on focus	Low: Marginally involved in the process, formerly a member of process team

Table 6.1: Leadership factors impacting group success

Does the discussion above mean that only managers can successfully lead computer-supported process improvement groups? The answer is, obviously, "no". If the answer were "yes", it would contradict at least one of the findings discussed in Chapter 5, which is that collaborative technology support decentralizes improvement initiatives. The evidence shows that a process owner does not necessarily have to be a manager for a group to succeed. For example, the group whose target process was *university course*, had as its leader a part-time graduate assistant, and was nevertheless a successful group.

It is important to note, however, that for a process owner not to be a manager, the process in question must be reasonably narrow in scope. And improvements in a process that is narrow in scope are unlikely to alone lead to radical gains from an organization-wide perspective. This type of process improvement is what business process reengineering proponents call *incremental* improvements (Hammer and Champy, 1993), and whose individual impact on the organization is small. However, the combined impact of such improvements has the potential to be bottom-line-significant, provided that they are obtained for a large number of processes in a more

Process description	Organization	Success	Perceived risk	Members' Interest in PI	Process involvement
Newsletter editing	MAF	High: Group agreed on process changes, from which all were implemented with positive results	Low: Problems and sources known to all members	High: Process problems affected all members	High: All members played roles in the process
University course	Waikato	High: Group agreed on process changes, from which all were implemented with positive results	Low: Problems and sources known to all members	High: Process problems affected all members	High: All members played roles in the process
Student assignment handling	Waikato	High: Group agreed on process changes, from which all were implemented with positive results	Low: Problems and sources known to all members	High: Process problems affected all members	Medium: Half of the members played roles in the process
International graduate student support	Waikato	High: Group agreed on process changes, from which all were partially or fully implemented with positive results	High: Racial, national origin, and other sensitive issues were discussed	Medium: Two thirds of the members were affected by process problems	Medium: Half of the members played roles in the process
International student adaptation support	Waikato	High: Group agreed on process changes, from which all were partially of fully implemented with positive results	Low: Problems and sources known to all members	High: Process problems affected all members	Medium: Half of the members played roles in the process
IT users support	MAF	High: Group agreed on process changes, from which three quarters were implemented with positive results	Low: Problems and sources known to all members	High: Process problems affected all members	High: All members played roles in the process
Software support	MAF	High: Group agreed on process changes, from which two thirds were implemented with positive results	Medium: Problem sources were unclear	Medium: Two thirds of the members were affected by process problems	Medium: Half of the members played roles in the process
Pest/disease outbreak communication	MAF	High: Group agreed on process changes, from which one third were implemented with positive results	Medium: Problem sources were unclear	High: Process problems affected all members	High: All members played roles in the process
Undergraduate academic support	Waikato	Medium: Group agreed on process changes, from which none was implemented	Medium: Some process info. was classified, problem sources were unclear	Medium: Half of the members were affected by process problems	Medium: All members played roles in the process, but roles and responsibilities were unclear
Quality management consulting	MAF	Low: No agreement on process changes was achieved	High: Executives' power and prestige at stake, problem sources were unclear	High: Process problems affected all members	High: All members played roles in the process
Staff training and development	MAF	Low: Unfocused discussion, the group was discontinued without agreeing on any process changes	Low: Problems and sources known to all members	High: Process problems affected all members	High: All members played roles in the process
Student computer support	Waikato	Low: No agreement on process changes was achieved	Medium: No agreement on problems, problem sources were unclear	Medium: Half of the members were affected by process problems.	Medium: Half of the members played roles in the process

Table 6.2: Membership factors impacting group success

or less synergistic way. The experience of the Japanese with incremental improvement initiatives between 1950 and 1980, shows that this can be achieved with spectacular aggregate results. A number of similar experiences in the U.S. after the 1980s also point in the same direction (Walton, 1989; 1991).

Membership factors

Table 6.2 shows the variation of membership-related variables along the twelve groups, as well as the degree of success obtained by each group. Groups are sorted by their degree of success, the most successful at the top and the least successful at the bottom. The three first columns of Table 6.2 are the same as in Table 6.1. The fourth column from the left shows the member perceptions trend for each group regarding discussion risk, that is, the degree to which careless computer-mediated contributions to the discussion were perceived by members as likely to negatively affect their careers. The two last columns show the members' general interest in the results of the process improvement attempt and the members' direct involvement with the process targeted for redesign.

An inspection on Table 6.2 suggests that the two membership-related variables that seem to consistently affect group success are *perceived risk* and *interest in PI*. With the exception of the group targeting the process *international graduate student support* at Waikato University, the five most successful groups had a low *perceived risk* and a high *interest in PI*. The variable *process involvement* was never low in any of the groups, moving somewhat erratically from high to medium along the twelve groups. Thus, no conclusions can be made regarding the relationship between this variable and group success.

This means that computer-supported PI groups are likely to be more successful if the perceived participation risk is low and the members' interest in the results of the process improvement attempt is high. A low perceived risk implies that either the discussion addresses no particularly "delicate" matters, or that there is enough trust among members so they can discuss any issue among themselves without fear of future back-stabbing. A high interest in the PI group's outcomes implies that most of those involved in the group have a stake in those outcomes - e.g. most members are directly affected by at least one of the problems identified with the process targeted by the group.

The perceived risk associated with actively participating in a PI group has been consistently seen as increased by computer support, according to the group members I interviewed. This is evidenced by the trend[2] of perceptions shown in Figure 6.1, which summarizes responses from forty-six interviews regarding computer support impact on perceived group participation risk. Fifty percent of the interviewees perceived computer support as having increased participation risk in their groups, while seventeen percent believed the opposite was true, that is, that computer support had in fact decreased participation risk.

The main reason given by interviewees to explain why computer support had, in their opinion, decreased participation risk was the relative isolation experienced

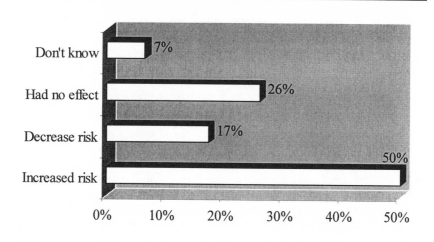

Figure 6.1: Distribution of perceptions about computer support impact on group participation risk

when contributing an electronic posting to the improvement group discussion. Apparently, these members were basing their explanation on the assumption that in a face-to-face situation other members could easily and immediately vent their disapproval or anger on them. In other words, they would be more at the mercy of other members in a face-to-face meeting than in the distributed and asynchronous virtual environment created by the computer mediation.

I interpret the perception trend by group members regarding the isolation enabled by computer mediation as a trace of a genetically programmed fear of violent reactions and personal confrontations in face-to-face interactions with other human beings. After all, we humans have had to rely on physical strength and the use of violence to survive and procreate during most of our evolutionary cycle. Some people (perhaps timid people) may feel the fear of face-to-face confrontation more intensely than others may. I therefore have some doubts as to whether this perception is rational, or even if it has anything to do with what can really happen in reality in the event of a conflict. Face-to-face confrontations within organizations rarely lead to physical threats or aggression, and are usually going to be "won" (though in many cases winning is not the most advisable strategy) by the person better prepared to handle an oral argument. In a computer-mediated confrontation, people may not have to face their interlocutors, and therefore may avoid immediate unpleasant feelings, but they will still have to face the consequences of their confrontation in the same way.

As for those interviewees who perceived an increase in participation risk as associated with computer support, their explanations to their interview answers seemed reasonably logical and rational. The majority of these respondents explained their answers by pointing out that computer-mediated communication leaves a record that can be kept by other group members for future use, and forwarded to many other people. In the words of one of these respondents:

The problem with [computer-mediated communication] is that it is very easy to think of it as a form of conversation, and yet it is also a written record, and people can easily write something down that they later regret. In a verbal situation, an oral situation, people tend to be a bit more accepting of people saying something inappropriate, and if they say something inappropriate often the cues of everyone else will protect them.

My interviews, participant observation, and interaction with group leaders suggest that two main situations are seen as risky in improvement groups. One of these is that in which the sources of process-related problems are not clear. In order to proceed with the group discussion, when this situation arises, some members must come forth and either admit that they or their departments (or teams) are causing the problems, or accuse other people of being the source of the problems. Either situation is obviously risky, especially since computer-mediation allows for the recording of whatever these people put forth. The other situation is that where classified or sensitive information (e.g. statistics that point to minority-related problems) has to be presented and openly discussed by group members. In the case of classified information, no group member may want to put forth the information in the first place. If someone does, it may be seen as a violation of the classified nature of the information, which is obviously a risky thing to do. In the case of sensitive information, those who provide the information as well as those who comment on the information may risk saying something that may be interpreted as inappropriate by other group members and people outside the group who got hold of a copy of the electronic posting.

The situations discussed above are, in my opinion, likely to arise quite often in improvement groups in general. However, I believe that they are more likely to happen in radical than incremental process improvement attempts. Radical improvement is usually targeted at broad, interdepartmental processes, which typically need urgent attention (Davenport and Stoddard, 1994). A large process breadth usually leads to several departments being involved in the process improvement effort. Urgency implies that there are big problems to be solved. The combination of these ingredients yields a process improvement effort dealing with big problems and involving several different departments. The likelihood that people from different, and often competing, departments will come forward and state in written that they admit being at the source of big problems is, in my opinion, very low (I am talking about normal, not kamikaze-like workers). One may argue that if there is enough *trust* in the organization, this may happen, but I have not seen this very often in my work with over fifty (computer-supported and otherwise) process improvement groups.

Group factors

Table 6.3 shows the variation of other group variables along the twelve groups. Again, as with tables 6.1 and 6.2, Table 6.3's rows are sorted by the degree of success obtained by each group; the most successful at the top and the least successful at the bottom. The three first columns of Table 6.3 are the same as in tables 6.1 and 6.2. The fourth column from the left shows the degree of complexity of the process targeted for improvement, which I assessed based on the assumption that it correlates the number of activities of the process and the perceived complexity of the process in the eyes of the group leader. The fifth column shows the breadth of the process targeted for improvement, which is proportional to the number of departments or distinct functions involved in the execution of the process targeted for improvement. The last column shows the group's departmental heterogeneity, which is proportional to the number of different departments represented in the group - i.e. if people from several departments were invited to participate in the process improvement discussion, then the group's departmental heterogeneity would be high.

No patterns can be inferred from the analysis of the most successful groups (top half of the table), as there is no predominance of "high" or "low" values for any of the three variables among highly successful groups. Yet, when one looks at the bottom half of the table, some patterns can be clearly identified. There is a prevalence of high target complexity and breath among the least successful groups. Four, among the five least successful groups, targeted processes of high complexity. Similarly, four out of the five least successful groups targeted processes whose breadth was high.

Although mainly qualitative and based on a relatively small sample, these patterns become significant when combined with other findings in this chapter

Process description	Organization	Success	Group's		
			Target complexity	Target breadth	Departmental heterogeneity
Newsletter editing	MAF	High: Group agreed on process changes, from which all were implemented with positive results	Low: Simple processes known to all group members	Medium: Interdepartmental	Low: 1 department (spread across 4 different sites)
University course	Waikato	High: Group agreed on process changes, from which all were implemented with positive results	Low: Simple processes known to all group members	Medium: Interdepartmental	Low: 2 departments
Student assignment handling	Waikato	High: Group agreed on process changes, from which all were implemented with positive results	Medium: Medium-complexity process, one third of the members knew the process well	Medium: Interdepartmental	Medium: 5 departments
International graduate student support	Waikato	High: Group agreed on process changes, from which all were partially or fully implemented with positive results	Medium: Medium-complexity process, one third of the members knew the process well	Medium: Interdepartmental	High: 8 departments
International student adaptation support	Waikato	High: Group agreed on process changes, from which all were partially of fully implemented with positive results	Low: Medium-complexity process, two thirds of the members knew the process well	Medium: Interdepartmental	Medium: 4 departments
IT users support	MAF	High: Group agreed on process changes, from which three quarters were implemented with positive results	High: Complex process, only one quarter of the members knew the process well	Low: Departmental	Medium: 6 departments
Software support	MAF	High: Group agreed on process changes, from which two thirds were implemented with positive results	Medium: Medium-complexity process, one third of the members knew the process well	Low: Departmental	Low: 1 department
Pest/disease outbreak communication	MAF	High: Group agreed on process changes, from which one third were implemented with positive results	High: Complex process, only one third of the members knew the process well	High: Whole business unit	Low: 1 department (spread across 6 different sites)
Undergraduate academic support	Waikato	Medium: Group agreed on process changes, from which none was implemented	Medium: Complex process, all members knew the process well	High: Whole business unit	Medium: 5 departments
Quality management consulting	MAF	Low: No agreement on process changes was achieved	High: Complex process, only one third of the members knew the process well	High: Whole business unit	Medium: 4 departments
Staff training and development	MAF	Low: Unfocused discussion, the group was discontinued without agreeing on any process changes	High: Complex process, only one quarter of the members knew the process well	Medium: Interdepartmental	Medium: 3 departments
Student computer support	Waikato	Low: No agreement on process changes was achieved	High: Complex process, only half of the members knew the process well	High: Whole business unit	Medium: 5 departments

Table 6.3: Other "group" factors impacting group success

regarding leadership and membership factors. They suggest that computer-supported process improvement groups targeting processes whose complexity and breadth are high are more likely to fail than are those targeting relatively simple and localized processes. As with leadership and membership factor patterns, the patterns emerging from Table 6.3 regarding groups' target (process) breadth point to incremental, as opposed to radical, process improvement groups as more likely to be successful when using computer mediation to conduct a large portion of their discussions. Low and medium-breadth processes are likely to involve either one or a few departments, but not a whole business unit, which makes their improvement less of a reengineering exercise than an incremental improvement one.

The interpretation of the high-process-complexity-low-group-success trend is not as straightforward. The perception that a process is highly complex does not depend only on the number of activities of a process. It also depends on how much a person knows about the domain area related to the process and her familiarity with the process itself. A process that looks simple to an electrical engineer (e.g. the design of the power infrastructure for a two-story house) may look very complex to a medical doctor. The opposite may be true for the process of operating an injured human knee. Thus, the evidence suggests, people who share knowledge about a given process are more likely to succeed in improving it in a computer-mediated fashion, even if the process is not that simple. That is, shared process knowledge may make a process look relatively simple to a group, even if the process does not look very simple to someone who does not know anything about it.

The discussion above suggests that groups whose members hold shared knowledge about a relatively narrow (i.e. low-breadth) process are likely to be more successful when improving the process in a distributed, asynchronous, and computer-mediated fashion. Obviously, these characteristics are quite likely to be found in process teams who, by definition, work on the same process and interact often (usually face-to-face). The problem is that, for these groups, asynchronous computer-mediation has very little use. Unless process team members work in different shifts, they can easily meet face-to-face, and thus will not probably be interested in meeting electronically.

The groups who can really benefit from distributed and asynchronous computer support are those which involve people from different departments, who can rarely meet face-to-face. These people do not share that much knowledge though. Yet, as Chapter 4 shows, the involvement of these people in computer-supported process improvement groups will lead to a buildup in their shared knowledge. In other words, people who engage in computer-supported process improvement tend to share knowledge, and this knowledge sharing is likely to increase the success of future groups involving the same members. However, until a certain amount of knowledge is shared, groups targeting "complex" (as perceived by most group members) processes may fail. Therefore, the wisdom apparently lies, as Buddha is believed to have said, in the "middle path" (as opposed to the extremes). Organizations should stimulate computer-supported process improvement groups to tackle processes of medium complexity and breadth, until employees are better equipped (with shared knowledge) to take part in groups targeting more complex processes (which, then, will no longer look so complex).

Incremental or radical improvement?

The discussion above indicates the following trends regarding the success of process improvement groups supported by an asynchronous collaborative technology.

- First, groups where the leader was the "owner" of the process targeted by the group were more successful than other groups.
- Second, groups whose discussion presented a low perceived risk to members and in which most members had a personal stake in the improvement of the target processes were more successful than other groups.
- Finally, groups whose target processes were broad and that were generally seen as complex by group members were less successful than other groups.

So, what does this tell us? Well, for once, it allows us to paint an idealized picture of a successful computer-supported process improvement group. Such group would have its leader as the owner of the target process, its discussion would present little personal risk for its members, and most of its members would have a personal stake in its outcome. Such group would also target a relatively narrow and simple process.

My experience facilitating incremental improvement as well as reengineering groups suggests that this idealized picture fits the "incremental improvement group picture" much better than it does what is usually known as the "reengineering group". The success factor analysis of the twelve discussed here, plus some of my previous studies of computer-supported process improvement (Kock and McQueen, 1995; 1998; Kock and Corner, 1997) strongly suggest, in my view, that collaborative technologies are most likely to succeed when used as a support tool for *incremental* process improvement groups. These groups should focus on relatively narrow processes (i.e. processes that involve a few departments in their execution), and be led by the individual responsible in the organization for those processes (who, I would like to emphasize, does not necessarily have to be a manager).

Can computer support be a trap?

Although generally positive, if used in the proper context, computer support can be a trap. This chapter discussed success factors, which can also be seen as factors whose absence may lead process improvement groups to fail. Several of the variables identified as being affected by computer support depend on an initial choice made by the group leader when selecting process-related problems and group members. For example, a choice of a problem such as "the design of our new products is not properly aligned with our marketing strategies" is likely to lead to a strategic-level choice of a process. A computer-supported group tackling such a process is likely to fail, if it tries to conduct a large amount of its discussion through an asynchronous collaborative technology, because of some of the reasons discussed in the chapter.

Among the myriad decisions a process improvement group leader may have to make, one specific type of decision can be particularly affected by the availability of collaborative technology support. The decision I refer to is the one related to who will participate in the process improvement group. The reason why computer support can negatively affect this decision is because computer support makes it very easy for *anyone* to participate in a process improvement group, even if that person has absolutely no interest in the outcome of the group.

The group whose target process was *student computer support* at one of Waikato University's colleges provides a good example of how computer support can be a trap when selecting group members. The self-appointed leader of this group was a graduate assistant who worked in one of Waikato's academic departments. This individual had previously worked as a computer support consultant, and was also familiar with process improvement activities. He gained support from the manager of the college's computer support division, who was eager to attain some strategic input from outside of his immediate support staff. He then went on to invite a number of faculty and staff, some holding senior-level positions, from five academic units to participate in the group. His main criterion for member selection was to invite people who had computer-related material in their course curricula. Most of those invited to become members agreed to participate immediately, apparently without much thought.

As shown in Table 6.2, this group was the least successful among the entire set of groups investigated. The group lasted thirty-two days. Seven members, from the eleven who initially agreed to participate, were active contributors (i.e. they wrote, as opposed to only reading, electronic postings) to the discussion. According to estimates provided by the group members, ninety-six per cent of the total time spent by group members in the group discussion was spent in interactions through the computer system. In the end, the group members achieved no agreement on process changes, and the group was generally considered a failure from a process improvement perspective. Some members pointed at the disturbing contributions of one particular group member, a senior faculty member at the college, as one of the reasons why this group failed. The referred group member had, among other things, allegedly addressed other members in a demeaning and sometimes offensive way. Later, in an interview, this member told me that:

I was a bit naughty, but I had already made my decision that [the group discussion] was not going to be effective, so I felt it was not going to be so much of a loss anyway. So, I basically, quite deliberately, upped the stakes by using phrases and language which were very exclusive, and quite controversial...It was my way of saying "You guys need to get a life, we need to move on because this is not going to work." It was the ultimate form of arrogance, if you want. I was playing a game.

During our interview, this particular group member declared having absolutely no interest in the improvement of the process itself, as he was not involved in the process in any way; neither as a client nor as a member of the team responsible for performing the process. He had decided not to be a client of the process, as some of his peers had, because he thought of himself as able to carry out the process activities himself. This was itself an indication that he was unhappy with the role the computer support division had been playing at his college. As an unhappy customer, he was initially seen as possibly a source of valuable input to the PI group. This obviously turned out to be a misassumption.

This example shows that the inclusion of some members, who would otherwise not participate in the group, may be facilitated by computer support. Although apparently beneficial, this may also become a trap for well-intentioned group leaders. Differently from computer-supported groups, face-to-face meetings may be disruptive to their members' personal schedules, forcing some of them to travel long distances, and leading some of them to cancel other important appointments. That is, there is personal *cost* to be met by those that accept to take part in a face-to-face process improvement group. Such cost may put off prospective members who do not have a high personal stake in the outcomes of the process improvement group, and thus induce a natural selection of the most interested individuals for the group. And, as discussed before in this chapter, a high personal interest in the outcomes of a process improvement group is likely to contribute to the group's success. Computer support often makes it initially very easy for people to participate in PI groups, which can lead to the inclusion of undesirable members.

Summary and concluding remarks

There is strong evidence that the current trends towards process improvement and organizational learning are going to carry on for quite some time, perhaps a few decades or more. We can also observe a trend towards what is know as the "virtual organization" paradigm. This picture implies that both process improvement and organizational learning will increasingly have to be carried out in a distributed, asynchronous, and computer-mediated manner.

Previous chapters discussed the relationship between process improvement and knowledge communication, which is one of the main components of organizational learning. The impact of asynchronous collaborative technologies on process improvement and learning was also discussed. What was missing is a discussion of success and failure factors in computer-supported process improvement groups, which is provided in this chapter.

Three main groups of factors seem to be associated with success and failure in computer-supported process improvement groups. These are *leadership*, *membership* and *group* factors. Leadership factors relate to characteristics of the leaders (or moderators) of computer-supported process improvement groups. Membership factors relate to group membership configurations. Group factors relate to general characteristics of each group, including characteristics of the target process.

Among leadership factors, the most closely related to group success was the process involvement of the group leader. That is, the more deeply involved the group leader was with the execution of the process targeted by her group, the better seemed the chances that the group would succeed. Among membership factors, the most closely related to group success were perceived risk and process improvement interest. That is, the more successful groups appear to be those in which there is little risk associated with active participation (as perceived by the majority of group members), and those in which most members are directly affected by process problems (and who thus have a personal stake in process improvement). Finally, among group factors, the most closely related with group success were target process complexity and breadth. There seems to be a prevalence of high target complexity and breath among the least successful groups.

The analysis of success factors allows us to paint an idealized picture of a successful computer-supported process improvement group. Such group would have its leader as the owner of the target process, its discussion would present little personal risk for its members, and most of its members would have a personal stake in its outcome. Such group would also target a relatively narrow and simple process. This idealized picture fits the "incremental improvement group picture" much better than it does what is usually known as the "reengineering group." Organizations should keep this in mind when embarking on computer-supported process improvement efforts.

Endnotes

[1] Or processes, as some groups targeted more than one process. See Appendix B for details on each individual group and the process or processes targeted for redesign.

[2] A chi-square analysis indicates that the probability that this trend is due to chance is around 1.5 percent, which suggests that the trend is statistically significant.

Chapter 7

Which Way Forward?

Information and knowledge explosion

The first electronic digital computer, the ENIAC, was developed in 1946 at the University of Pennsylvania, in Philadelphia, with funding from the US Army. By then, computers were seen as giant calculators, capable of performing thousands of complex mathematical operations per second. As World War II had just been over, and the prospect of a global nuclear race was looming large, one of the main applications of computers at that time was ballistics calculation. Computers would allow for the calculation of warhead missile trajectories with both high speed and unprecedented precision.

The situation above has slowly changed in the 1960s and 1970s, with the development of smaller and cheaper computers, and the first attempts to set up large area networks linking several computers. This period has seen the development of ARPANET, the precursor of the Internet, by the U.S. Department of Defense. One of the components of ARPANET, and by no means the most important component at the design time, was an application called electronic mail (or, simply, *email*). In spite of the fact that ARPANET's main goal was to allow scientists spread throughout the U.S. to share computer resources (mostly mainframe computing power), the single most successful of ARPANET's components was, surely enough, *email*. This was a first hint that information and knowledge sharing were becoming more pressing needs than the distributed use of computer processing power. Computers were starting to be seen as communication support and data storage tools, rather than just incredibly fast number crunchers.

The 1980s have seen the widespread use of the microcomputers, particular IBM PC compatibles, and the first successful commercial network operating systems. As previously mentioned in Chapter 1, one of the most successful companies in the development of local area network operating systems at this time was Novell Corporation, a Utah-based company. Their Netware operating system presented two basic attractions to organizational customers. The first was the ability to allow several users to share what were then relatively expensive computer peripherals, such as laser and color printers, over the network. The second was to enable data sharing among users, which means that users were able to share data files and applications over the network. The Netware operating system allowed data and peripherals sharing in an almost seamless way. It carved a new information technology market, and opened the way for a number of other similar products.

Computer networks became ubiquitous in the 1990s, with the emergence of new and cheaper network operating systems. A major player in the stand-alone operating systems market, Microsoft Corporation, launched three operating systems with built-in networking capabilities, for a fraction of Novell Netware's price. These operating systems were dubbed Windows for Workgroups[1], Windows 95, and Windows NT. As a result, computer networks became commonplace at organizations of all sizes. These were major steps in connecting computers, and therefore people, through local are networks (LANs). However, these networks involved computers located usually in the same building. A major breakthrough came with the development and widespread use of the Internet, largely propelled by the development of the World Wide Web in 1991, the first Web browsers in 1993, and the emergence of Internet service providers (ISPs). ISPs provided access to the Internet to non-governmental companies and individual users. With the advent of the Internet, physical location was no longer an issue, and it became easier for organizations to set up wide area networks (WANs).

The picture above is not complete without a brief discussion about the explosion of information and knowledge available for the production and delivery of goods and services (see chapters 3 and 4 for a more detailed discussion on this). Information is eminently descriptive. It describes the world as it is, as well as changes in its components. Therefore, two main sources of new information are new *discoveries* about the world that we live in[2], as well as *changes* in this world. There is no general agreement about how much information is generated, but since the pace of new discoveries and global change have been both accelerating at least since the early 1900s, it is reasonable to assume that more and more information is created every day.

Of course, new discoveries mean new knowledge, and as the pace of research increases in different fields, so does the pace with which knowledge is created in these fields (of course, we are assuming that research usually leads to new knowledge, but not that all research does so). And, at least one of my previous studies shows, beyond much doubt, that the number of different experts involved in carrying out a process is proportional to the number of information exchanges in the process (Kock et al., 1997). That is, knowledge fragmentation correlates information flow. Also, as discussed in Chapter 4, knowledge fragmentation into different fields of expertise is a direct consequence of the explosion in the amount of existing knowledge, as human cognitive limitations lead human beings (who cannot store too much knowledge about too many things) into knowledge specialization.

From the above, it is fair to conclude that there is a pressing need for large amounts of information to be exchanged among people in organizations, and that this need is increasing everyday. It is also reasonable to conclude, mostly based on the historical discussion of the use of computers, that computer networks are being and are likely to keep on being the basic infrastructure through which information is exchanged[3]. In this environment, organizations *will have to* muster techniques to make distributed, computer-mediated work (i.e. routine process execution) happen in an efficient *and* effective way. Moreover, as organizations will have to continuously improve themselves and adapt to change, this will also have to be carried out in a distributed, computer-mediated fashion. Below I present and discuss some approaches to how this can be done, based on the discussion presented in previous chapters.

Distributed improvement and learning

Previous chapters presented a relatively optimistic view of the effects of computer support on distributed process improvement groups. The range of effects discussed can be placed into three main categories— group process effects, group outcome effects, and effects on organizational learning.

Group process effects refer to the (*meta-*)process of conducting distributed process improvement groups, and the related effects of computer support. The evidence presented and discussed in previous chapters indicates that computer support causes a reduction of *group set up time* and *group demand for senior leadership*. A lower group set up time leads to lower *group duration*. Finally, the combination of a decrease in group duration and in group demand for senior leadership leads to an increase in the possible *number of simultaneous groups* that can be conducted at any organization at a given time.

As for group outcomes, the evidence discussed so far in this book is generally inconclusive regarding significant positive or negative effects. The evidence indicates a generally neutral, and certainly non-negative, trend of perceptions regarding group outcome quality. This is due to three main primary effects of computer support. The support provided by the computer system appears to have increased *group departmental heterogeneity*, measured as the number of different departments represented in a group, and *member contribution quality*, perceived as the general quality of individual computer-mediated contributions in a group. Computer support was also seen as associated with an increase in *discussion ambiguity*, or the likelihood that individual computer-mediated contributions by members would be misunderstood by others in the group.

The combination of the primary effects led to a neutral effect on group outcome quality, but that was not so for organizational learning. The same primary effects discussed above led to an increase in organizational learning. Two types of evidence support this finding. The first type are perceptions of group members, provided in interviews, about their individual learning in computer-supported groups in comparison with similar face-to-face groups. The second type were the counts of knowledge exchanges in improvement and routine processes.

As a whole, the findings just discussed are generally positive. They are summarized in Figure 7.1, which provides an integrated view of all the computer support effects discussed in this book. The bottom-line effects are shown on the right-hand side of the figure, which includes the effects on the main dependent[4] variables identified in my study. These are *number of simultaneous groups* and *organizational learning*, which are both increased by computer support. Also a main

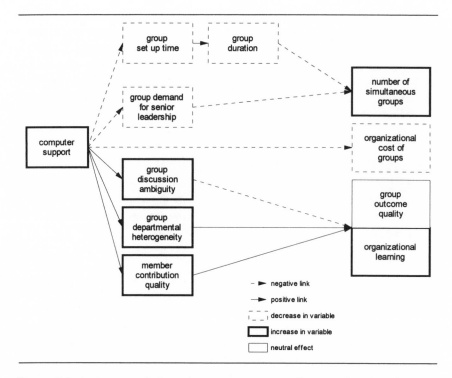

Figure 7.1: An integrated view of computer support effects on distributed process improvement groups

dependent variable is *organizational cost of groups*, which is decreased by computer support. The fourth and final dependent variable is *group outcome quality*, which is unaffected by the computer support.

Primary and secondary effects on intervening variables (all the other variables in Figure 7.1, except *computer support*) mediate the effects on the main dependent variables. Arrows connecting variables in the models represent these effects. A dotted arrow represents a negative effect, that is, one in which an increase in the variable on the left contributes to a decrease in the variable on the right. A solid arrow represents a positive effect, that is, one in which an increase in the variable on the left contributes to an increase in the variable on the right. Variable changes are represented through the border of the rectangles in which they are contained. A thick border means an increase in the variable; a dotted border means a decrease; and a regular border means that the variable is unaffected.

It is very important, however, that the model in Figure 7.1 be interpreted in light of the group patterns discussed in Chapter 6 regarding success and failure factors in computer-supported distributed process improvement groups. The findings summarized in the causal model suggest that more simultaneous process improvement groups will be conducted if distributed computer support is available, and that conducting these groups will be less expensive for an organization than conducting similar face-to-face groups. The model also suggests that group outcome quality is not going to be affected and that organizational learning will be increased.

However, whenever a process improvement group fails, the gains above are not actually realized; at least, not to their full potential. Who cares if process improvement becomes cheaper because of computer support, if it is unsuccessful? If this is the case, it may be better not to run a process improvement group in the first place, unless substantial organizational learning gains are achieved. And, there is no clear evidence that the amount and quality of learning experienced by group members can offset the losses (e.g. wasted time) caused by an unsuccessful process improvement effort. In fact, my own direct observation of process improvement groups indicates that group failures are seen by most group members as simply *failures*, irrespective of how much members learn as a result of the group discussion. The main reason for this is probably because process improvement groups are set up to accomplish process improvement, not knowledge sharing. If the main goal of *process improvement* is not achieved, group members will see their group as a failure and, in consequence, may not want to take part in future computer-supported process improvement groups.

Therefore, management must take some precautions when promoting computer-supported process improvement in their organizations, despite the generally positive impact of computer support on distributed process improvement groups. Such precautions are presented and discussed below, organized as a set of prescriptions for organizations.

Some recommendations for organizations

There is a large number of organizational recommendations that can be derived from what was discussed in previous chapters of this book. But, since the reader of this book is probably more interested in a synthesis at this stage, rather than another dose of analytical arguments, I will be as brief as possible without lacking much completeness. I believe my prescriptive comments can be summarized into three main items, discussed below.

* The leader of a process improvement group should be deeply involved in the execution of the target process. He or she should, ideally, be the process owner. This does not mean that the group leader should be a manager, but implies that if the leader is not a manager, the scope of the target process should be relatively limited. This feature is more likely to be found in incremental process improvement groups than in reengineering groups.
* Computer-mediated discussions should not be used alone in broad scope, radical process improvement groups (i.e. reengineering groups). Because of the high perceived risk and process complexity involved in such groups, face-to-face meetings are a must in these cases. Computer support can be used to conduct *part* of the group discussions, particularly to summarize and provide a record of what was discussed face-to-face.
* Only people who have a stake in the outcomes of a process improvement group should be invited to participate. Group leaders should make sure that members whose interest in process improvement is only marginal are not included in the group. The same is true for members who do not want process changes to take place, and who could therefore sabotage the group discussion. This is particu-

larly important in computer-supported groups, as there is evidence suggesting that disruptive or undesirable behavior is more difficult to handle electronically than face-to-face.

In my opinion, most computer-supported process improvement groups will be successful if the above recommendations are followed. This will occur without major losses in the benefits of computer support. I assume that a group methodology similar to the one discussed in Appendix A is followed, which itself involves a number of further normative components (e.g. criteria, prescriptions, guidelines, graphical tools).

The recommendations above do not involve major modifications in organizational culture. This is probably a major advantage of these recommendations over the more broad culture-oriented prescriptions so often found in the popular management literature. Changes in organizational culture are notoriously difficult to implement. However, it is useful to examine how the creation of an organizational culture that is conducive to computer-supported process improvement and organizational learning could be accomplished.

Creating a conducive organizational culture

The popular business literature is filled with suggestions implying that organizational cultures that promote "trust" among their members are the ideal ones to stimulate process improvement and organizational learning. Case studies are presented portraying some companies as unbelievably trusting and friendly environments, apparently devoid from any sign of internal animosity or competition. These companies are often presented as the most successful in their industries, a paragon to be venerated and imitated. Many readers are so marveled at these stories that they become priests of the new gospel, trying to replicate the same environment in their own organizations. I must admit that I was one of such converts at a certain point of my consulting career.

However, my own experience has often contradicted the idea that organizations can be turned into extremely safe, friendly and trust-oriented environments, even when top management encourages this culture through incentives and personal example. The problem seems to have its roots in the fact that we live in a competitive environment, and this is taught to us since our early years and throughout our lives. Kids compete for grades in school, for prizes in local sport competitions, and even for the right to be left alone by other bullish kids. And, could this be any different? After all, we are animals that evolved through Darwin's natural selection, a *highly* competitive process itself. It is reasonable to expect that this is in some way ingrained in our genetic code as a species, and that this guides to a large extent our own behavior.

Other organizational development approaches argue that we should avoid the fragmentation of knowledge and work, which perniciously pushes people into becoming part of common-interest groups and isolating themselves from people outside these groups. Sometimes I think that those who propose these and similar approaches are very smart, because they probably know that they will never be proven wrong. Since it is impossible to avoid knowledge fragmentation and work specialization, unless we find a way to stop the (seemingly unstoppable) knowledge and information explosion, the organizational cultures prescribed by these so-called "management gurus" will never be fully implemented. When faced with failures to prevent knowledge and work fragmentation, the gurus will always be able to say, as many of them do, that *"You haven't done it quite right...not exactly as I said."* After all, if what someone is saying can never be tested, then the person can never be proven wrong.

I do believe that some things can be done to promote a culture oriented toward process improvement and organizational learning. However, we have first to accept some organizational realities:

- Most people will keep on aggressively competing for everything, particularly in countries that promote competition as a way of life like the U.S. and many others. Thus, organizations will have to figure out alternatives to use individual competitive drive to promote synergy among separate organizational functions. In fact, most organizations do not have to push people into being more competitive. They would be better off easing the demand for aggressiveness. Releasing pressure on individuals will probably reduce individual stress and increase productivity, without any curbing effect on competitive behavior.
- The trend toward knowledge and work fragmentation is an irreversible one, and will continue its accelerated march into the future. Therefore, organizations will have to find ways to bring experts together in collaborative efforts, as opposed to trying to turn everyone into a generalist.
- Finally, computer technologies will be ubiquitous, and most computers will be networked, whether they are within or outside traditional organizational boundaries. This will lend new meaning to the term "virtual organization." Practically anyone who has access to the Internet from home, can also reach (and be reached by) work colleagues from (at) home. Telecommuting and work from home will become more and more common. Geographical organizational barriers will be less and less an issue in the implementation of interdepartmental processes. Therefore, companies will have to learn how to implement and use computer support tools for distributed work.

Organizational problems, or illnesses, have been traditionally attacked using approaches that resemble those of conventional medicine. That is, prescriptions are handed by "organizational doctors" (usually management consultants) to be followed by managers and employees with the expectation that the problems will be eliminated.

However, some clinical fields adopt a different approach. In these fields, the first step that clinicians take to fight body illnesses is to *educate* the patients about their illnesses. By transferring specialized knowledge to patients, doctors help the patients help themselves, and prevent the recurrence of former habits that were contributing to the disease. This is particularly true for illnesses that are caused by complex brain processes, whose chemical dynamics is not yet very well understood. Clinical psychologists and psychiatrists, for example, have long found that some psychological disorders can be effectively treated through educating their patients about the cause of the disorders, with little or no chemical treatment.

In a way analogous to learning curing psychological illnesses, I believe learning can be used to improve organizational norms, habits and culture. People should understand the nature of their aggressiveness, and how it can be harnessed to produce positive individual and organizational results. Organizations should also promote management and worker's understanding of such concepts as "processes" and "knowledge." The trend towards knowledge fragmentation and its organizational consequences should be understood. Based on this, efficient approaches should be devised to convince people that they should know something about what others do, particularly process teammates. Finally, prospective members of process improvement groups should understand how computer support could affect their groups.

Summary and concluding remarks

Previous chapters discussed several issues regarding the impact that collaborative technologies have on process improvement and organizational learning. These can be briefly summarized as:

- An increase of the number of simultaneous process improvement groups that can be conducted at an organization.
- A decrease of the organizational cost of process improvement groups.
- A neutral effect on group outcome quality.
- An increase in the organizational learning, reflected in the perceptions of members of process improvement groups.

However positive the above findings may sound, they can only become reality if some precautions are taken by organizations. These can be summarized in the three following guidelines.

- Process improvement group leaders should be deeply involved in the execution of the target process. They should, ideally, be the process owners. Leaders do not, however, need to be part of the management staff at organizations.
- Computer-mediated discussions should not be used alone in broad scope, radical process improvement groups (i.e. reengineering groups). Computer support can be used to conduct *part* of the group discussions in these cases.
- Only people who have a stake in the outcomes of a process improvement group should be invited to participate.

Finally, computer-supported process improvement and organizational learning will be best accomplished if it is rooted in a conducive organizational culture. Such culture can be built by educating organizational members about process improvement's mechanics and its likely results. Efficient approaches should be devised to convince people that they should know something about what others do, particularly process teammates. Finally, prospective members of process improvement groups should understand how computer support could affect their groups.

Endnotes

[1] Windows for Workgroups was seen and called by many as an operating "environment", rather than a full-fledged operating system. This was because it needed, as its predecessor (the stand-alone Windows), the Microsoft DOS operating system to be run. Windows for Workgroups carried out most of its functions by making system calls to Microsoft DOS.

[2] These include discoveries about us, our body and our mind, and about how we behave individually and in groups.

[3] Note that I am not talking here about *knowledge* exchanges because I do not think that much knowledge is in fact exchanged in current organizations, or that current information technologies contribute much to knowledge communication. Obviously, I think they should, and this is one of the main points I try to make in Chapter 4.

[4] Dependent variables are the most important variables in a cause-effect model such as the one discussed here. The effects on these variables usually summarize whatever causal relationships exist in a model.

Appendix A

Using MetaProi to Improve Processes

MetaProi at a glance

In my discussion of process improvement and organizational learning, I have shown that process improvement has the potential to foster inter-functional knowledge communication and, in consequence, organizational learning. In Chapter 4, I have analyzed process improvement efforts that led to levels of knowledge communication not normally seen in routine organizational processes. These process improvement efforts have all been carried out through process improvement groups.

Given the potential advantages for organizations from conducting process improvement groups, the issue of how to conduct such groups gains importance. There are a number of "how-to" texts on process improvement. Such texts describe a variety of normative approaches. Classic texts on how to improve process quality have been written by Crosby (1980; 1984), Deming (1986), Ishikawa (1986), and Juran (1989), and fed the "quality fever" of the 1980s. Popular texts focusing on the improvement of process productivity have been written by Davenport (1993), Hammer and Champy (1993), Hammer and Stanton (1995), and Harrington (1991), and fed the "re-engineering fever" of the 1990s.

In this appendix I propose my own approach for process improvement, named MetaProi, which by necessity is based on the texts just described as well as other related books and papers. A previous book presents a preliminary discussion of this approach (Kock, 1995a). MetaProi's focus is both quality and productivity, and was designed so it could be conducted through electronic as well as face-to-face meetings. One example of an electronic discussion based on MetaProi is provided at the end of this appendix.

MetaProi is a group methodology for process improvement. One of its components is a group process (or meta-process). As a methodology, MetaProi can be fully defined as a set of activities, guidelines, criteria and graphical tools to be used by process improvement groups. It is suggested that group size should be between three to twenty-five participants who play the roles of group leader, facilitator, and ordinary member. The group goal is to identify an organizational process where improvement opportunities exist, and propose changes in order to translate those opportunities into practical improvement.

MetaProi is short for Meta-Process for Process Improvement. It is referred to as a "meta"-process to indicate that it is a high-level process which describes how process improvement is carried out in organizations. MetaProi is made up of three main stages: process definition, analysis, and redesign. Each stage comprises interrelated activities. In order to define the criteria, guidelines, and tools to be used in MetaProi, it is important to identify the activities in each of the stages, as well as the group roles involved. Group roles in MetaProi are analogous to process functions in organizations. The activities involved in each of the stages are summarized below:

- *Process definition (Definition stage)*:
  Identify problems.
  Identify processes.
  Select a process for redesign.

- *Process analysis (Analysis stage)*:
  Model the process.
  Raise performance information.
  Highlight opportunities for improvement.

- *Process redesign (Redesign stage)*:
  Search for suitable changes.
  Incorporate changes to the process model.
  Evaluate redesign feasibility.

An illustration of MetaProi as a set of interrelated activities is provided in Figure A.1. Arrows indicating the flow of data briefly describe the outputs and inputs of the activities.

The illustration in Figure A.1 is a simplification of the real process. The goal of this illustration is to provide a clear yet limited view of MetaProi as a whole. Loops and interactions with members outside the group are not represented, though these are likely to occur in real process improvement groups. For example, a group may decide, while performing the activity "evaluate redesign feasibility", that it must go back to the activity "search for suitable changes", due to the impossibility of implementing some of the proposed changes. Also, the facilitator of a group targeting a specific process in the IT Department of an organization may well need, in the stage "raise performance information", information from the Finance Department.

Two permanent groups should be set up by an organization implementing MetaProi in order to guarantee the success of process improvement groups: the Process Improvement Committee and the Process Improvement Support Team. The Process Improvement Committee analyses process redesign proposals and, when necessary, coordinates and supports their implementation and standardization throughout the organization. Process Improvement Committee members should have

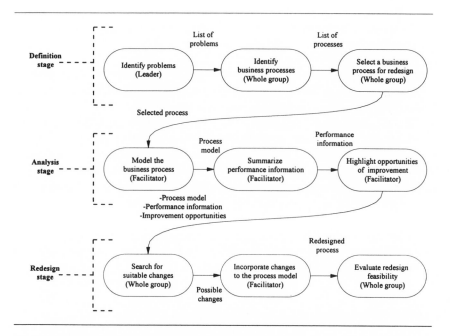

Figure A.1: MetaProi as a set of interrelated activities

enough authority to coordinate the implementation of strategic changes, such as those requiring large investments and organization-wide restructuring.

The Process Improvement Support Team's main function is to provide process improvement groups with necessary methodological and technological support. It is also responsible for documenting, organizing, and providing public access to the information about process improvement initiatives in the organization (e.g. documents and electronic postings generated by previous process improvement groups).

Group roles in MetaProi

MetaProi comprises only three group roles: leader, facilitator, and member. A process improvement group is initiated by a self-appointed leader, who should initially identify a set of related problems to be tackled by the group. The group leader then invites other members to be part of the group, and appoints one of these members as the group facilitator. The group leader should advise the Process Improvement Support Team that the group has been created, so it can support and document the group's evolution.

The leader coordinates the activities of the group and interacts with the Process Improvement Support Team. The responsibilities of a group leader include:

- Scheduling meetings and making sure the necessary resources are available. Such resources may include a room and overhead projector, or an electronic conferencing system.
- Contacting group members and making sure they are able to attend the group meetings, either face-to-face or electronically.

- Gathering and organizing the documentation generated by the group and, after the process improvement group has completed its work, supplying the Process Improvement Support Team with this documentation.

In a process improvement group the facilitator is responsible for creating and maintaining a model of the process targeted for redesign. This model is generated according to one of the process views discussed in Chapter 2.

The facilitator is also responsible for summarizing performance information about the process, and for highlighting opportunities for improvement. These responsibilities demand a thorough understanding from the facilitator about MetaProi's criteria, guidelines, and tools. However, the facilitator does not decide alone on the adoption of specific changes. This is a prerogative of the process improvement group as a whole and must be obtained by consensus.

The other members of the group (i.e. the "ordinary" members) will provide their inputs throughout the group discussion in a "low cost" participation mode. As in most types of moderated group discussions, most of the burden is on the leader and facilitator. One person can play more than one role in the group, e.g. one person can be the group leader, the facilitator, and provide inputs as a group member.

General guidelines for MetaProi

Some guidelines that relate to the whole process improvement meta-process and which are not associated with a particular activity are:

- The process improvement group should come up with a redesign proposal in a limited amount of time. This should be no more than eight weeks. Previous research shows that an acceptable average time is three weeks (Kock and McQueen, 1995).
- The several stages a process improvement group goes through should be documented. The leader is primarily responsible for this documentation, which is essential to build up the historical information about organizational process improvement initiatives. This information can be used for many purposes, such as a basis for future process improvement groups, and as evidence of the organization's commitment to improving process quality in quality accreditation audits (Kock and McQueen, 1997). For example, the organization may use process improvement group documentation in ISO-9000 certification audits to show that it follows exemplary procedures for dealing with "non-conformities".
- Each of the group meetings should conclude with a link to the next meeting. A meeting where the activities "identify problems" and "identify processes" are accomplished should end with a preliminary selection of a process to be redesigned. This preliminary selection works as a link to the next meeting, where the first activity will be "select a process for redesign." These "links" between meetings are aimed at improving group focus.
- The facilitator should not try to enforce the group process described in this guide, that is, MetaProi. He or she should rather induce it in as transparent a way as possible. This will occur almost naturally, as the facilitator will be responsible for several of the key activities of the process improvement group.

Activities in MetaProi

The following subsections provide a discussion of each of the activities in MetaProi, including criteria, guidelines, and tools used. Subsection titles are formed by the main stage, which is followed by a colon and the name of the activity.

Definition stage: Identify problems

In the definition stage, the first group activity is to identify problems. As discussed before, the person who first brings the problems up for discussion is a self-appointed group leader. Virtually anyone can be a group leader, which helps spread the responsibility for the innovation over the organization, as well as reduce innovation's reliance on managers. This broadens process improvement's scope of application, as the number of managers in one organization is usually smaller than that of line employees.

In some forms of process improvement, where the improvement is gradual and accomplished by permanent groups (e.g. quality circles), the search for improvement does not necessarily rely on previous identification of problems. In these cases the improvement is routinely sought, based on the assumption that every process can always be improved in one way or another. However, research shows that the identification of problems, as sources of discontent within the organization, is a success factor in process improvement (Hall et al., 1993).

The identification of problems fosters interest in process improvement among organization members and, at the same time, gives them an idea of what is to be achieved with the improvement. The identification of problems, though, is only the beginning of MetaProi. The main outcome of MetaProi is process improvement, not problem solving. The identification of problems is an intermediate step that leads to the selection of a process for improvement (Harrington, 1991).

A list of interrelated problems should first be generated and then submitted to the process improvement group so mistakes and omissions can be corrected. The group leader should prepare the preliminary version of the list. This is the first step in the formation of the group. Concurrently with the generation of this list, the leader should invite prospective group members. Listing problems and inviting group members are two interrelated tasks. Little involvement can be expected from group members who have no interest in the problems initially listed.

Problems in the list should be at least intuitively related. A list of problems that is excessively broad, involving several different areas, for example, leads to the identification of several processes for redesign. This is likely to disperse the focus of the process improvement group.

Problems should be approached in a very clear and open way. There should be no fear of disclosing discontent with the actual situation. Poor identification of problems (e.g. certain problems are not discussed because they may upset some individuals) leads to poor process redesign (Deming, 1986; Kock and Tomelin, 1996).

Definition stage: Identify processes

Once a list of interrelated problems is identified, the next step is to identify the processes causing those problems. At this point it may be found that some processes are clearly defined, while others are not (Wastell et al., 1994).

However, the process improvement group should not try to build process models in this activity. Instead, it should try to describe in one or few words the interrelated activities that are perceived by the group as the causes of the list of problems. For example, if a company specializes in performing financial audits, the problems listed may be "late invoices," "customer complaints about invoice complexity," "inaccurate invoices" and "late payment." As these are all related to the auditing service, the processes can be simply described in this activity as "invoicing" and "auditing." Later, in the second stage of MetaProi —the process analysis stage - the selected process or processes will be analyzed in more detail.

The relationship between problems and processes is a many-to-many one. Several processes can cause one problem and, conversely, several problems can be caused by one process. Thus, even though the initial list of problems may have only one problem, it may help in the identification of several processes for improvement.

Definition stage: Select a process for redesign

This activity is a conclusion of the work started in the previous activity, the activity identify processes. Here one of the processes identified in that activity will be chosen for redesign.

When several processes are identified, group members may want to select more than one process for improvement. This is frequently the case when there are no clear boundaries between processes within the organization. However, as the number of selected processes increases, so does the complexity in the next stage, that is, process analysis. An additional drawback of a group selecting many processes for redesign is the high number of changes likely to be proposed by the group. A high number of processes selected for redesign may hinder the process improvement group from focusing on one specific process that needs urgent attention. It may also reduce the level of care given to the analysis and redesign of each individual process.

Criteria
- The process improvement group should strive to select as few processes as possible. Ideally, only one process should be selected.
- The process that is associated with the most critical problems should be given priority in the selection.
- After applying the preceding criteria, the process that is associated with the highest number of problems should be given priority in the selection.

Analysis stage: Model the process

In this activity the process considered for improvement by the process improvement group is modeled according to one or more of the views discussed in Chapter 2. Each view implies a type of process representation, of which I will discuss the flowchart (workflow view) and the data flow diagram (data flow view). The goal of this activity is to understand the relationships between process activities, as well as to achieve a clear view of the process as a whole.

Graphical tool: Flowchart

Flowcharts have been extensively used in the past to represent processes, especially from an information systems analysis and design perspective. Davis (1983) describes a flowchart by defining sixteen symbols used as its basic units. Harrington (1991) states that "Flowcharting [...] is an invaluable tool for understanding the inner workings of, and relationships between, process" (pp. 86) and discusses five types of flowcharts:

- *Block diagram.* This is the simplest type of flowchart and uses only two symbols.
- *American National Standards Institute (ANSI) standard flowchart.* This type of flowchart is more elaborate than the block diagram. Harrington (1991) suggests a list with twelve standard symbols to be used with this type of flowchart.
- *Functional flowchart.* This flowchart uses the same set of symbols as the ANSI standard flowchart. It also includes a horizontal grid describing the functions in the activities as roles.
- *Functional time-line flowchart.* This flowchart adds some extra information to the functional flowchart, including information about the processing and cycle time of each of the activities.
- *Geographic flowchart.* This flowchart describes where activities physically take place and how functions and products move within the organization during their execution.

I will describe and use the ANSI standard flowchart. Yet, for simplicity, I will use only four symbols. These symbols are slightly modified to condense more information than in the ANSI standard. This simplification was adopted in a previous study by me (Kock, 1995a) where several manufacturing and service processes were modeled. The four symbols used are illustrated in Figure A.2.

The symbols listed in Figure A.2 are meant to be a minimal list to be used for process representation. Such simplification has also found widespread acceptance in some organizations, such as Ford and Volkswagen, in process descriptions for their corporate quality manuals (Kock, 1995a). A discussion of the symbols in Figure A.2 is provided as follows:

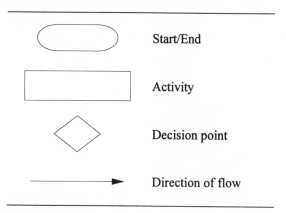

Figure A.2: Flowchart symbols

- *Start/End*: Used to show the beginning and end of a process. Normally, the word "start" (in the beginning of the process) or "end" (in the end of the process) are included within this symbol.
- *Activity*: Used to represent an activity within the process. A brief description of the activity is provided within this symbol, together with a description of the function responsible for the activity and the main artifact used (e.g. activity: drill a batch of network cards; function: drill operator; artifact: numeric-controlled drill).
- *Decision point*: Used to show that at a certain point in the process a decision must be made. The groups of activities executed after a decision point will vary according to the decision made at the decision point. Typically, decision point symbols are marked with a set of options, which describe where the activity flow

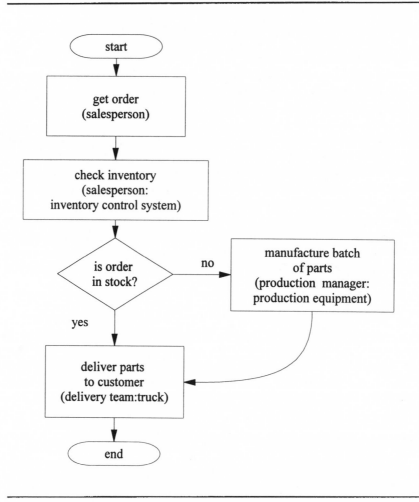

Figure A.3: Example of flowchart

should proceed after the decision (e.g. yes-no; true-false; option 1, 2 or 3).
* *Direction of flow*: Used to indicate the direction of the activity execution flow within the process. Arrows linking pairs of activities indicate the direction of flow. ANSI suggests that the arrowhead is not necessary when the direction flow is obvious (e.g. from top to bottom).

An example of a simple process modeled with the use of the symbols described above is provided in Figure A.3. This example was adapted from an illustration in Kock (1995a, p. 149) describing a generic order fulfillment process for an automobile part manufacturer.

Each process flowchart should be accompanied by a written description of the most important activities, highlighting information that may be useful in the redesign stage. This description should also include information that is not explicitly represented in the flowchart. For example, it is not clear from the flowchart in Figure A.3 how the production manager is informed that a batch of parts needs to be manufactured.

As discussed in Chapter 2, a flowchart diagram usually leaves out one of the most important components of a process, that is, its data flow. Even when the flow of data is included in a flowchart, usually going from one activity to another, it is a misrepresentation of the real data flow in the process. The main reason is because data do not flow between activities, they flow between process functions. A type of diagram that is particularly suitable for showing how data flow is the data flow diagram, discussed next.

Graphical tool: Data flow diagram

Data flow diagrams (DFDs) have found widespread use in organizations, particularly due to the widespread adoption of structured analysis and design techniques for the development and deployment of information systems in organizations in the 1970s and 1980s (Davis, 1983; DeMarco, 1979; Pressman, 1987). However, DFDs have not been traditionally used to support process analysis and redesign. They have been typically used to understand processes and automate the processes "as they were". That is, it has been traditionally used for analysis, but not redesign.

Different types of DFDs have been proposed in the late 1970s and widely used since. Notable contributions have been made by DeMarco (1979), Gane and Sarson (1979), as well as Yourdon and Constantine (1978). The DFDs proposed by these authors differed mostly in the shape, basic function, and number of symbols used in the diagrams. Later, Ward and Mellor (1985) proposed an extended set of symbols to be used in DFDs representing "real-time" systems (e.g. continuous process control systems).

For convenience, I will describe and use a type of DFD that I have developed by amending a previously suggested notation, and used in most of my consulting and teaching practice. This DFD uses a set of symbols that is not much different from that proposed by Gane and Sarson (1979). The general meaning of the symbols used is virtually the same. The symbol set used is shown in Figure A.4.

As with the symbols used in flowchart diagrams, I believe the symbol set in Figure A.4 is enough to provide a nearly complete representation of the flow of data

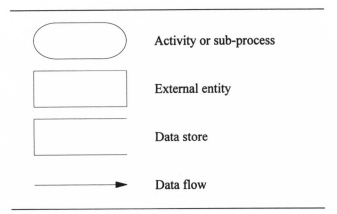

Figure A.4: DFD symbols

in a process, with relatively little effort from the process modeler. The meaning of the symbols shown in Figure A.4 is:

- *Activity*: Used to represent an activity or sub-process within the process being modeled. As with the activity symbol in flowcharts, this symbol typically comprises a brief one-to-two-word description of the activity along with brief descriptions of the organizational function responsible for the activity and the main artifact used.
- *External entity*: Used to represent a source or recipient of data flowing in a process. A brief description of the function receiving or supplying data is provided within this symbol.
- *Data store*: Used to represent a data repository, which may take forms as varied as a computer file or database, an inbox, an electronic mailbox, a fax folder, or a billboard. A brief description of that data stored is provided within this symbol.
- *Data flow*: Used to describe the data components flowing within a process. As discussed before, data flow between organizational functions, as well as from these to data stores and back. A data flow is described with an arrow pointing to the direction of the flow, along with a brief textual description of its main component.

A simple example of DFD is provided in Figure A.5. The process represented is same as in Figure A.3, that is, a generic order fulfillment process for an automobile part manufacturer. The difference is that Figure A.3 is a flowchart representation of the process, whereas Figure A.5 is a DFD representation.

A comparison of figures 3 and 5 highlights some of the usual differences between DFDs and flowcharts. Although the DFD in Figure A.5 contains descriptions of the same activities (or sub-processes), it also incorporates descriptions about how data flow within the process modeled. DFDs typically provide a richer representation of processes, particularly in processes in which a lot of data have to be stored and transferred.

Given the above-mentioned characteristic of DFDs, it should come as no surprise that they are my preferred graphical representation for process modeling. However, this opinion does not find much agreement among process modelers,

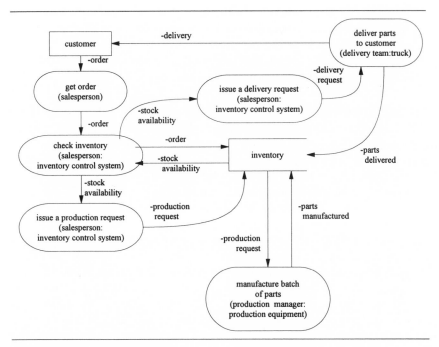

Figure A.5: Example of DFD

particular those engaged in business process re-engineering. A preferred approach among this group is the use of activity-based diagrams, with special attention devoted to the use of IDEF0 representations1.

Guidelines

*   The description within the activity symbols should be as brief as possible and begin with a verb in the infinitive form (e.g. drill a computer card, load a batch of parts onto a truck).
*   Flowcharts and DFDs should have a limited number of symbols in order to avoid excessive complexity. Studies on human cognition limitations provide the basis for establishing an optimum number of symbols in process modeling diagrams (Miller, 1956). These studies suggest that this number should be between five and nine symbols (i.e. 7 plus or minus 2). When a process cannot be represented with less than fifteen symbols (i.e. twice the optimum average), due to its complexity, some of its activities should be "exploded" into lower-level DFDs (Pressman, 1987).
*   Trivial artifacts should not be described in activities (e.g. pen and paper, telephone). A rule of thumb is to describe only artifacts that are specific to an activity type and without which the activity cannot be carried out (e.g. lathe, computerized drill, cheese processor, inventory control system). An artifact is specific to an activity type whenever it has been designed to support only that type of activity.
*   When modeling a process, the facilitator should not be afraid of adding

handwritten notes and marks to the diagram if they are needed to clarify certain points. The emphasis should be on using the graphical tool in an effective way (i.e. to convey information that will allow the group to redesign the process) rather than in an efficient way (i.e. keep the chart as neat and tidy as possible by strictly sticking with the flowcharting symbolism).

Analysis stage: Summarize performance information

In this activity, information about the performance of the process is summarized for the process improvement group. This information should gravitate around two main process attributes: quality and productivity. A direct measure of process quality is customer satisfaction, so the best way to evaluate it is to obtain information on how the customers of the process perceive its outputs.

The customers of a process are those in and outside the organization who receive products generated by the process. These products can be services, goods, information, or computer software. Lathe operators, for example, are customers of a lathe maintenance process. The maintenance service they are provided with also affects the quality of the products generated by the lathe operators themselves.

Productivity is traditionally measured by the ratio outputs/inputs (Misterek et al., 1992). This means that a car assembly process that employs ten workers and produces two cars per hour may be said as of having a productivity of $2/10 = 0.2$ cars per hour per worker. If the same process is redesigned so it can produce the same two cars per hour, but now with five workers, then its productivity will be $2/5 = 0.4$ cars per hour per worker. That is 100% higher than before.

However, a better way to measure process productivity is by considering the ratio (production capacity)/(production costs). This offers two advantages against the (input/output) approach discussed in the previous paragraph:
• It considers the costs of the inputs to the process, and not their quantity; and
• It takes into consideration the capacity of a process, and not its realization.

The quantity of each input may remain the same even when its cost is reduced due to process improvement. For example, the process related to the production of hamburgers can benefit from a smarter purchase of bread, whether the number of bread units is reduced or not. This is why the analysis of cost is critical to productivity measurement, as opposed to the approach of counting the number of inputs. Yet, this approach implies a higher measurement complexity, as costs can vary considerably with time.

The measurement of the production capacity for a process implies forecasting. To say that a car assembly process has a production capacity of three hundred cars a day means that the assembly line can manufacture on average that figure, but not that it is the real average output. Since production in real contexts depends on consumption expectancy, which in turn is based on sales orders or forecasts, the simple measure of outputs can lead to wrong assumptions about productivity. This risk is suppressed when productivity assessment is based on production capacity (Goldratt and Fox, 1986). Complexity here is, again, increased by the need to estimate process output capacity based on historical figures and resource capacity of specific units (e.g. the production capacity of a machine in a manufacturing plant).

However, in many cases this may be easier than relying on real numbers whose measurement is severely hampered by the added cost of extensions in the accounting system of the organization (Mark, 1984).

So, I generally believe that the analysis of productivity should be based on estimates of production capacity and costs, rather than on outputs and inputs. While likely to add complexity to measurement, this is useful in that it draws a line between productivity and quality assessment. The output/input approach disregards the fact that quality improvement is bound to generate more consumption, and consequently promote an increase in output (Deming, 1986). By connecting productivity with the actual outputs produced by a process, one could mistake quality for productivity improvement. This is particularly true when a surge in demand due to higher quality is simply supported by excess capacity, not augmented productivity.

Guidelines

- In the first activity of MetaProi, the one aimed at identifying problems, the group should have gathered information on user complaints. In this activity, the facilitator should try to find quantitative data associated with those complaints. He should try, for example, to identify, by means of quantitative measures, the problems customers see as most critical, and those that occur most often.
- The facilitator should not be concerned, in this activity, with generating performance information. The facilitator should, instead, focus on summarizing existing information about the process performance. This information may come from areas of the organization that are not represented in the process improvement group. Generating performance information may take too long and, therefore, make the process improvement group lose momentum. A lack of process performance information, identified by a group in its analysis stage, may become a problem to be tackled by a different process improvement group.

Analysis stage: Highlight improvement opportunities

In this activity, the facilitator will highlight opportunities for improvement, based on performance information raised in the previous activity. This is helpful to lead the process improvement group towards the discussion of concrete changes to improve the process.

Guideline

The facilitator should highlight process improvement opportunities by proposing changes in the process to be discussed by the group. These changes should be based on the information gathered during the two previous activities, namely "model the process" and "raise performance evaluation". They should also follow the guidelines discussed in the next activity, that is, "search for suitable changes".

Redesign stage: Search for suitable changes

In this activity group members will propose suitable changes in the process so improvements of quality and productivity can be achieved. The literature on process improvement provides several guidelines for improving processes. These guidelines can help process improvement group members formulate their redesign proposals.

Guidelines

Harrington (1991) provides several guidelines for process improvement based on general principles such as process and activity simplification, bureaucracy elimination, standardization, and technology utilization. Hall et al. (1993) and Venkatraman (1994) propose guidelines for redesigning processes according to improvement dimensions and scope levels. Guha et al. (1993) and Wastell et al. (1994) present some process improvement guidelines as part of specific process redesign programs. Dingle (1994) and Caron et al. (1994) draw guidelines from the analysis of process reengineering cases.

In my own work, I often opt for splitting process improvement guidelines into three main domains of process improvement, namely information flow, structure of activities, and management system. I did so as part of a process improvement methodology named PROI, which stands for PROcess Improvement (Kock, 1995a) and served as a basis for MetaProi. Some of these guidelines that may be useful within the context of MetaProi are listed below:

- *Foster asynchronous communication.* When people exchange information they can do it synchronously, i.e. interacting at the same time, or asynchronously, i.e. interacting at different times. One example of synchronous communication is a telephone conversation. If the conversation takes place via e-mail, it then becomes an example of asynchronous communication. It has been observed, especially in formal business interaction, that, almost always, asynchronous communication is more efficient. For example, synchronous communication often leads to time waste (e.g. waiting for the other person to be found) and communication tends to be less objective. Asynchronous communication can be implemented with simple artifacts such as in-and out-boxes, fax trays, and billboards. These artifacts work as dynamic information repositories.
- *Eliminate duplication of information.* Static repositories, as opposed to dynamic repositories, hold information in a more permanent basis. A student file maintained by a primary school, for example, is a static repository of information. Duplication of information in different static repositories often creates inconsistency problems, which may have a negative impact on productivity and quality. In my previous book (Kock, 1995a), I describe a situation where a large auto maker's purchasing division tried to keep two supplier databases updated; one manually and the other through a computer system. Two databases were being kept because the computer database had presented some problems and therefore was deemed unreliable. This, in turn, was causing a large number of inconsistencies between the two databases. Each database stored data about over four hundred parts suppliers.
- *Reduce information flow.* Excessive information flow is often caused by an over-commitment to efficiency to the detriment of effectiveness. Information is perceived as an important component of processes, which drives people to an unhealthy information hunger. This causes information overload (Toffler, 1970) and the creation of unnecessary information processing functions within

the organization. Information overload leads to stress and, often, the creation of information filtering roles. These roles are normally those of aides or middle managers, who are responsible for filtering in the important bit from the information coming from the bottom of, and from outside, the organization. Conversely, excessive information flowing top-down forces middle managers to become messengers, to the damage of more important roles. Information flow can be reduced by selecting the information that is important in processes and eliminating the rest, and by effectively using group support and database management systems.

- *Reduce control.* Control activities do not normally add value to customers. They are often designed to prevent problems from happening as a result of human mistakes. In several cases, however, control itself fosters neglect, with a negative impact on productivity. For example, a worker may not be careful enough when performing a process activity because he knows that there will be some kind of control to catch his mistakes. Additionally, some types of control, such as those aimed at preventing fraud, may prove to be more costly than no control at all. Some car insurance companies, for example, have found out that the cost of accident inspections, for a large group of customers, was much more expensive than the average cost of frauds that that group committed.

- *Reduce the number of contact points.* Contact points can be defined as points where there is interaction between two or more people, both within the process and outside. This involves contacts between functions, and between functions and customers. Contact points generate delays and inconsistencies and, when in excess, lead to customer perplexity and dissatisfaction. In self-service restaurants and warehouses, for example, the points of contact were successfully reduced to a minimum. Additionally, it is much easier to monitor customer perceptions in situations where there are a small number of contact points. This makes it easier to improve process quality.

- *Execute activities concurrently.* Activities are often executed in sequence, even when they could be done concurrently. This has a negative impact primarily on productivity, and is easier to spot on process flowcharts and DFDs. In a car assembly process, for example, the doors and other body parts can be assembled concurrently with some engine parts. This has been noted by several automakers, which, by redesigning their processes accordingly, significantly speeded up the assembly of certain car models.

- *Group interrelated activities.* Closely interrelated activities should be grouped in time and space. Activities that use the same resources, i.e. artifacts or functions, may be carried out at the same location and, in some cases, at the same time. I often illustrate this point using the case of a telephone company which repaired external and internal house telephone connections (Kock, 1995a). This company had two teams, one team for internal and another for external repairs. An internal repair occurs, by definition, within the boundaries of a commercial building or residence; external repairs involve problems outside these boundaries. Whenever the telephone company received a customer complaint, it used to send first its internal team. Should this team find no internal connection problem, the external team would then be dispatched check the problem. It took a process improvement group to show the company that it was wasting thousands of dollars a year, and upsetting customers due to repair delays, by not combining the two teams into a single repair team. This was because, when complaints were categorized and counted, it was found out that most of the problems were external.

- *Break complex processes into simpler ones.* Complex processes with dozens (hundreds in some cases) of activities and decision points should be "broken" into simpler ones. It is often much simpler to train workers to execute several simple processes, than one complex process. It is also easier to avoid mistakes in this way, as simple processes are easy to understand and coordinate. In support of this point, I discuss in (Kock, 1995a) the case of an international events organizer, which was structured around two main processes: organization of national and international events. After a detailed analysis of these two processes, which embodied over a hundred activities each, it was found that they both could be split into three simpler sub-processes: organization of exhibitions, conferences, and exhibitors participation. This simplification improved the learning curve for the processes, as well as reducing the occurrence of mistakes. It did not, however, lead to an increase in the number of employees needed. The reason is because, with simpler processes, one person could perform functions in various processes at the same time.

I would like now to make one important comment about this activity. Here, process improvement group members should not be so concerned about the feasibility of their redesign proposals. This concern will only limit the innovativeness of the redesign, and therefore its effectiveness. Redesign feasibility analysis will be carried out at a later point, in an activity included especially for this purpose.

Redesign stage: Incorporate changes into the process

In this activity, the facilitator should incorporate the changes proposed by the group into the process flowchart or DFD and respective written description. This new process model works as a feedback to the group, so proposed changes can be refined.

Guideline

The facilitator should try to state at this point who would be responsible for implementing the proposed changes in the process. If such changes need involvement from higher management levels this should be clearly stated. Such involvement may be needed, for example, for investment approvals and certain changes in the organizational structure.

Redesign stage: Evaluate redesign feasibility

This is the last activity of MetaProi. In this activity the group members should discuss the feasibility of the changes proposed to the process so far and, if necessary, modify them to adapt those changes to the reality of the organization.

Subsequent stages: Implement and refine redesign

The next stages are the initial implementation of the changes, and their refinement, so they can be used in a routine way and perhaps in other similar organizational processes. The group can proceed on its own to these stages, provided that no involvement from higher management levels is necessary to implement the changes. If enough authority to approve and support the changes proposed can be found within the group, for example, and so do the resources to carry this implementation out, then the group can proceed to process change implementation right away.

If the above is not the case, the group should submit the change proposal to those who are in a position to have it implemented. Ideally, this should be done through the Process Improvement Committee, which is the committee responsible for the evaluation of redesign proposals and coordination of their implementation.

MetaProi in practice: A college example

The following example shows parts of a discussion carried out by a process improvement group to improve a process. The discussion takes place in a fictitious college, and the process tackled relates to a practical introductory course to information systems. The course's name is Introduction to Business Computing; course code 0127A. The course had two theoretical classes per week, as well as ten laboratory practical sessions altogether. This discussion is based on a real discussion, which took place in a similar context. Names and situations have been disguised to protect confidentiality.

The discussion shown here was performed with the use of an electronic mail system, and was led and facilitated by a person referred to here as Angus. Angus was also the tutor of the introductory course that was targeted by the process improvement group. Other group members were John, Anne and Mark, who were faculty members involved in the design and teaching of course 0127A; Phil and Linda, who were members of the college's computer support staff; and Paula, who was director of the college's Computer Support Division, and boss of Phil and Linda.

Definition stage: Discussing problems

Angus selected and invited the six college members above to join the process improvement group. He did so based on several problems he had identified during course tutorials. Group members were invited via telephone, electronic mail, and face-to-face conversations. They were given a description of the topic of the discussion and the group process to be followed, that is, MetaProi. All those invited agreed to take part in the process improvement group. The discussion was then started, as proposed in MetaProi, with a message sent by Angus to all process improvement group members, describing the main problems observed during course tutorials. In the same message, Angus pointed out main causes for the problems and asked the group members for comments. This message is shown next:

From:	Angus
To:	John, Anne, Mark, Phil, Linda, Paula
Date:	6 June 1995 1:04pm
Subject:	0127A Course Problems (please give your feedback)

In the first semester several problems contributed to lower the quality of the 0127A course (Introduction to Business Computing). In this message I try to identify the main problems found and what might have caused them. I might have forgotten something or mistaken certain causes, so please send your comments to either me or all the recipients of this message. Any contributions will be appreciated, including criticism.

The goal of this discussion is not to find someone to blame. It is to improve the quality of the course.

List of main problems observed in the first semester:
-Students seemed to be, in general, upset by the workload. They complained that the course had too many assignments and that they were too time consuming.
-From prac 5 on, the students didn't seem to understand what they were doing. Several students reported that these pracs were too "mechanical".
-There are several minor mistakes in the manual, for all the pracs (annotated by me).
-The sample files created for pracs 9 & 10 (using the software MS Access) don't fit on most of the computer HDs at the labs. Most of these computers have less than 2 Mb available on C: drive. The sample files created are above 1.5 Mb. This leaves very little working space for the operating system, which in turn starts to issue strange error messages.
-Meetingworks (prac 4) didn't work properly, even after more than 7 previous tests where problems were found and supposedly solved.
-Trader (prac 8) doesn't load sample files in the network. If you create the files on one machine, these files cannot be used on another machine. Platinum Software and Computer Support Division were contacted, but no solution was found so far. Platinum software says Trader was not designed to run on a network.
-MS Access (pracs 9 & 10) was not configured to be used on the network. Certain functions (e.g. Wizards and print definition) cannot be used by more than one student at the same time.
-Several hardware problems in the lab, such as: mice that don't work, print queues that don't match actual printers, machines that are too slow, and (mainly) print server breakdowns.

Possible causes for the problems:
-*The way pracs were designed*. Again, I'm not trying to blame anybody. I think that the redesign of the pracs, keeping the problems above in mind, is one way to improve 0127A course quality.
-*The way communication is carried out today, between Computer Support Division and the lecturers*. For example, some pracs were designed assuming that the HDs in the lab had enough capacity. As there always are constraints in a process (e.g. resources that are likely to create problems) their identification is very important so further problems can be avoided. The way communication has been done so far does not foster the identification of those constraints.
-*The way the Computer Support Division handles requests*. I don't have knowledge of workload and how internal activities in the Computer Support Division are carried out, but I feel the consequences (e.g. requests

take too long to be fulfilled, and recurrence of failures). Some of these consequences may well be caused by external causes (e.g. unbalance between resources and demand). A discussion of this point may require a separate thread, since I and the lecturers in this improvement group are not the only Computer Support Division customers.

Please give your feedback focusing on the problems and possible causes described above ASAP. As it is important that we concentrate our improvement efforts in one of the causes only, I'd like to ask you to choose one cause to be tackled by this group. This cause can be chosen from the list above or another suggested by a group member.

Angus

Angus, in his first message above, set the main lines of the discussion comprising the three first activities of MetaProi, namely Identify Problems, Identify Processes, and Select a Process for Redesign, which are the activities of the first stage of MetaProi, the Definition Stage. Below are a few of the replies from group members.

From: Anne
To: Angus, John, Mark, Phil, Linda, Paula
Date: 7 June 1995 12:20pm
Subject: 0127A Course Problems (please give your feedback) -Reply

Interesting to hear about your experiences; I do a lot of my teaching in the lab. The general thrust of your comments matches my experience -no matter how hard you try to set up modules, assignments etc to run 100% smoothly, there always seems to be problems.

Some of the problems are avoidable, some less so. Possibly your database assignment can be done with a database a lot smaller than 1.5mb? There does seem to be an inordinate number of operational problems in the lab - mice not working, won't read disk drives etc - at any time at least half a dozen PCs (in part) seem to be u/s for one reason or another.

Lotus has run very solidly for my courses in the last Semester - WP6 has been a bit wobbly at times; MS Access collapsed for everyone on a couple of occasions but since then an update has been installed and it has been behaving. I don't use Trader but getting the network/ standalone business sorted out is obviously important.

I find the Computer Support Division to be pretty good and getting better. One of my problems is that my classes are 5-7pm on two nights, so if technical problems arise in the lab, its difficult for me to get rescued.

Despite the frustrations for both teacher and students, I feel that the overall value in raising students' computer literacy more than offsets this
Hope these comments help.

Anne

From: Mark
To: Angus, John, Anne, Phil, Linda, Paula
Date: 7 June 1995 1:48pm
Subject: 0127A Course Problems (please give your feedback) -Reply

1. I don't think the assignments were too much. Perhaps the pracs were too time consuming. We need to reduce the tasks. The tasks were mechanical on purpose - to facilitate marking. I don't see another way considering the resources we have.

2. Hardware/software problems. We just need to fix them. There are bound to be some hiccups with a course of this nature.

Mark

From: John
To: Angus, Anne, Mark, Phil, Linda, Paula
Date: 8 June 1995 11:39am
Subject: 0127A Course Problems (please give your feedback) -Reply -Reply

Anne's comments match my own experience but I don't think we are going to get anywhere trying to solve technical problems. Those are the Computer Support Division's responsibility. I think we should concentrate, as a group, on the way pracs are designed and run.

John

From: Paula
To: Angus, John, Anne, Mark, Phil, Linda
Date: 9 June 1995 12:18pm
Subject: 0127A Course Problems (please give your feedback) -Reply -Reply

I agree with John's comments and think that we could discuss some of the problems initially listed by Angus in another group at Computer Support Division. I recognize there are problems in our Division and am open to suggestions of improvement.

I think that in this group, though, we should concentrate on the way pracs are run.'

Paula

Analysis stage: Summarizing information

The discussion summarized in the messages above pointed towards the process embodying the activities involved in designing and running the laboratory sessions (also referred to as "pracs") as the process to be improved by the group. Based on this, the facilitator sent the following message to the process improvement group:

From: Angus
To: John, Anne, Mark, Phil, Linda, Paula
Date: 12 June 1995 12:50pm
Subject: 0127A Course Problems (an analysis of the process)

Thank you all of you who contributed with comments on the problems found in the 211 course.

Anne and Mark surveyed student's perceptions both half way and at the end of the course. In this message I summarize the results of those surveys and add a flowchart model of the process of designing and coordinating 0127A pracs. Based on it and on the discussion so far, changes are proposed. Please add new changes or correct those that you think are inappropriate or will not work. I'll send you a third an final message within a few days with a list of the agreed changes. These changes will be then implemented and their results will be evaluated during the next semester.

Summary of surveys (perceptions of the pracs only):
 -The pracs provided practical and relevant grounding in using computers.
 -There was too much work compared to other courses.
 -There should be more tutorials and less pracs.
 -There should be more lab times available.
 -There should be more tutors in labs and prac marks should be returned faster.
 -Prac labs were noisy and cramped.

Flowchart model of the process of designing and coordinating pracs:
Please find the model attached. In order to read it, go to the option "view", choose the option "zoom" and then "zoom area". Then just select the area to be viewed in the flowchart[2].

Summary of proposed changes (and those who would be responsible for them):
 -In looking for activities in the flowchart that could be done at the same time or concurrently, I and John realized that a good deal of the markings could be done during the lab. This will probably reduce the amount of printouts per class and, consequently, the effect of print server breakdowns (Angus).
 -Simplify pracs in order to reduce workload (tutor & course lecturers).
 -1)Move pracs 4 (Meetingworks), 9 and 10 (MS Access) to other labs outside the college, to a private course provider. or 2)have the problems with Meetingworks and MS Access sorted out here (Phil, Linda, and Paula).
 -Change the exercises for prac 8 (Trader), so the students have to enter their own sample data to work with (John).
 -Check the applications used in the 0127A course in all the machines in the lab, every week, to make sure they are working properly (Phil and Linda). Angus would give in advance, to the Computer Support Division, a list of applications to be used in each week of the next semester .
 -Attach control cards to the machines so the students report problems and know the configuration of the machines and their previous history of problems (Paula).

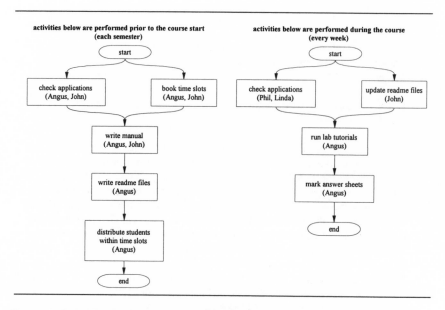

Figure A.6: 0127A Course Processes Model

The feedback from the members of this group to this message will define which changes will actually be put in practice. Send your input as soon as possible.

Thanks,
Angus

In his message above, Angus, the facilitator, provides the background for three activities of MetaProi, namely Model the Process, Summarize Performance Information, and Highlight Opportunities of Improvement, which are the activities of the second stage of MetaProi, the Analysis Stage. Below are a few of the replies from group members.

From: Phil
To: Angus, John, Anne, Mark, Linda, Paula
Date: 12 June 1995 2:41pm
Subject: 0127A Course Problems (an analysis of the process) -Reply

Angus
a couple of comments on your mail message

1 on moving to use an outside lab several points
a it will cost you
b i don't think you'll find someone with Meetingworks
c some of the MS Access problems we have are documented Microsoft problems of which they have no solution in a network environment...

2 on checking apps being used.. it is already computer support policy that

the labs are checked prior to a class if the course booking the lab communicates its intentions

Phil

From: Anne
To: Angus, John, Mark, Phil, Linda, Paula
Date: 13 June 1995 5:09pm
Subject: 0127A Course Problems (an analysis of the process) -Reply

Angus,

I think it will be hard for you to mark assignments in the lab, during the prac. You have your hands full helping these people. Marking is going to take a lot of extra time. I don't think you will have the time during lab hours.

Anne

From: Angus
To: John, Anne, Mark, Phil, Linda, Paula
Date: 14 June 1995 6:57pm
Subject: 0127A Course Problems (an analysis of the process) -Reply
-Reply

Anne,

In your message you say that I won't have time to mark assignments during the lab prac. That's a good point. However, in analyzing the process of running the pracs I realized that I get rushed off my feet mainly due to two reasons: 1)system problems and 2)complicated exercises. The main source of system problems are server problems, which seem to occur more often when the print queues are flooded with a large number of jobs (which is what normally happens when approx. 35 students try to print at the same time). In marking only those exercises that ask for printouts, hence waiving the respective printouts, I believe I may even reduce the rush during prac slots, since there will be less problems (not to mention the damaging effect of these problems to the image of the college). I'm not completely sure, though, this will happen.

The second reason, complicated exercises, is expected to have its impact mitigated with the simplification of the pracs.

Angus

Redesign stage: Selecting and evaluating changes

The process improvement group, after discussing the possible changes proposed by the facilitator and proposing new alternatives, clearly leaned towards some possible changes. The facilitator summarized these changes, in the message below, sent to the members of the process improvement group. In this message, the facilitator also asks the group about the completeness and appropriateness of the changes, that is, an evaluation of the redesign feasibility.

From: Angus
To: John, Anne, Mark, Phil, Linda, Paula
Date: 16 June 1995 4:56pm
Subject: 0127 Course Problems (changes aimed at improving the pracs)

Thank you all those who contributed with comments on how to improve 0127A course pracs.

Below is a summary of proposed changes based on our previous discussion. Please send your feedback on this summary to the discussion group (recipients of this message). Please let us know if you think some of the changes are inappropriate or the summary is not complete.

<u>Summary of changes to be implemented (together with an indication of those who are responsible for their implementation):</u>
 -Mark in lab, during the time slot, those exercises that ask for printouts. In these cases the printout will be waived when the student shows a suitable "print preview" (tutor).
 -Reduce workload in pracs - specifically at pracs 5, 6, 7, 9 and 10 (tutor and lecturers).
 -Have MS Backup, or other backup program, easily accessible to the students so they can store large files (Computer Support Division).
 -Solve Trader sample files problem (already implemented by Computer Support Division).
 -Try to reduce the size of the sample files used at pracs 9 and 10. In case it's not possible, book another lab (the new lab that has been just built) for those pracs (tutor).

Angus

Angus, in his message above, provides the background for three activities of MetaProi to be performed. These activities are Search for Suitable Changes, Incorporate Changes into the BP Model, and Evaluate Redesign Feasibility, which are the activities of the third stage of MetaProi, the Analysis Stage.

Note that Angus did not provide another graphical representation of the process, since the changes in the process did not lead to changes in the flowcharts. This was because the flowcharts did not represent the process in much detail. The evaluation of the redesign feasibility was performed as the replies of the group members were discussed. Some few of those replies are shown bellow.

From: Linda
To: Angus, John, Anne, Mark, Phil, Paula
Date: 17 June 1995 8:33pm
Subject: 0127 Course Problems (changes aimed at improving the
            pracs) -Reply

Angus,

Given the context of you message I assume the purpose of backup is to store large files??...if this is the case there are better and easier (more reliable options - you may wish to discuss this with me).

Linda

From: Angus
To: John, Anne, Mark, Phil, Linda, Paula
Date: 18 June 1995 5:07pm
Subject: 211 Course Problems (changes aimed at improving the
           pracs) -Reply

Linda,

  The purpose of backup is primarily to give students access to a tool for
backing files up. Storing large files is a desirable spin-off.
  If you think there are better options, please choose the best among them
and let me know how the students can use it. I've got no preference for MS
Backup.

Angus

From: John
To: Angus, Anne, Mark, Phil, Linda, Paula
Date: 19 June 1995 5:07pm
Subject: 211 Course Problems (changes aimed at improving the
           pracs) -Reply

I've already discussed some of the changes to reduce the workload in the
pracs with Anne and Mark. I think it can be done without compromising the
learning content. We are going to carry it out right away.

John

From: Paula
To: Angus, John, Anne, Mark, Phil, Linda
Date: 20 June 1995 5:07pm
Subject: 211 Course Problems (changes aimed at improving the
           pracs) -Reply

I agree with the changes concerning the Computer Support Division. By the
way, the problem with Trader, which has already been solved, as noted by
Angus, was caused by the configuration of the network. Printing with
Trader, though, is still impossible (at least to network printers). An alternative is to print to a file (most of Trader options allow it) and use Notepad or
Wordperfect to print the file to a network printer - these programs work well
on the network.

Paula

This marked the end of the process improvement group discussion. The
discussion shown here was summarized (e.g. not all messages were shown) and
targeted a simple set of problems. The process improvement sought was a local one,

and involved non-strategic processes. Authority to carry out the proposed changes and the respective resources needed were entirely found within the group. These changes were subsequently implemented and led to quality and productivity improvements that were seen as remarkable in the eyes of most group members.

Summary and concluding remarks

This appendix discussed MetaProi, a group methodology for process improvement. MetaProi comprises a set of activities, guidelines, criteria and graphical tools to be used by process improvement groups. It assumes that groups will have from three to twenty-five participants, who perform three main roles: (a) group leader, (b) facilitator, and (c) ordinary member. One person can play more than one role in the group, e.g. one person can be the group leader, the facilitator, and provide inputs as an ordinary group member. The group goal is to identify an organizational process where improvement opportunities exist, and propose changes in order to translate those opportunities into practical improvement.

MetaProi is made up of three main stages: process definition, analysis, and redesign. Each stage comprises the following interrelated activities.
• Definition stage:
    • Identify problems.
    • Identify processes.
    • Select a process for redesign.
• Process analysis (Analysis stage):
    • Model the process.
    • Raise performance information.
    • Highlight opportunities for improvement.
• Process redesign (Redesign stage):
    • Search for suitable changes.
    • Incorporate changes to the process model.
    • Evaluate redesign feasibility.

Each activity incorporates criteria, guidelines, and(or) graphical tools for its effective completion. This appendix lists these, categorized by activity. It also shows how many of them can be put in practice, through an example of a successful process improvement group.

Endnotes

[1] IDEF0 is the activity-based graphical modeling tool of the IDEF modeling standard. IDEF, in turn, stands for Integrated Computer Aided Manufacturing Definition. One of the reasons IDEF0 has been widely used in process modeling has been its early adoption as a standard process-modeling tool by the US Department of Defense (DOD) and other US government departments.

[2] These instructions were designed for users of Groupwise, which was the computer system used to support the group discussion. The flowchart model is provided in Figure A.4 and contains two, rather than one, closely related business processes.

Appendix B

A Close Look at Twelve Process Improvement Groups

Introduction

In this appendix, I provide a description of each of 12 process improvement groups conducted at MAF Quality Management and Waikato. These descriptions and other group information have been used in analyses discussed in previous chapters. Each group description comprises:

(1) Motivation: This item describes why the group was conducted. Here, I describe general problems faced by the organizations that called for improvement. I also describe related pressures faced by prospective group leaders, which motivated them to undertake improvement initiatives.

(2) Formation: This item includes how the group was begun and who were invited to take part in the group discussion.

(3) Features: This item includes general features of the group such as duration, total number of members, number of members who posted at least one electronic message to the group, number of electronic postings exchanged by members, and proportions of total time spent by members interacting electronically and orally.

(4) Stages: This item describes how the group stages of process definition, analysis and redesign were conducted.

(5) Results: This item describes the outcomes of the group discussion in terms of actual process improvement and short-term organizational implications.

MAF.G1: Software support

Motivation

MAF Quality Management's regional information technology support department was established to provide general information technology support to MAF

Quality Management's offices located in New Zealand's North Island. Such support typically involved the solution of hardware and software problems upon request from the users, and preventive upgrades in the region's information technology infrastructure, including local connections and local area networks' operating system software.

Recently, the department had been receiving a number of complaints from users, particularly relating the departmental process of providing software support for users. Three main problems, from the users point of view, appeared to be at the source of those complaints:

- A perceived slow turnaround of software repair jobs.
- A lack of information about the "status" of their jobs — i.e. requests for software application repairs.
- A high number of problems related to their local area networks, seen as likely being caused by the department's limited time to carry out preventive local area network software maintenance.

Formation

One of the department's team leaders decided to lead this group and invited four other employees of the same department to take part in the discussion. Two of the invited members worked in the same office as the group leader. Their organizational seniority was slightly lower than the group leader's. One of the other members was the acting regional manager of the information technology support department, the group leader's boss, whose office was about 100 meters down the hall in the same building as the group leader's. The fourth prospective member was based in a different city and was subordinate to the group leader. All those invited agreed to participate in the discussion.

Features

The group lasted 28 days and comprised five members from only one department, and based in two different cities. From the five agreeing to participate, only three members contributed postings to the discussion. The interaction in this group comprised seven electronic postings, and a number of one-on-one phone and face-to-face conversations.

According to estimates provided by group members, 83 percent of the total time spent by group members in the group discussion was in interactions through the (e-mail conferencing) EC system, whereas the remaining 13 percent was in oral one-on-one interactions.

Stages

In the definition stage, the group leader posted a message to the group containing a list with three problems and two processes, suggested as the main causes of the problems and thus as the target for the redesign. This posting was followed by two replies with comments on the leader's message. These replies led to the selection of one process for redesign.

In the analysis stage, the leader posted a message to the group containing a textual description of the selected process, a summary with performance-related information and eight proposed changes. This posting was followed by 2 replies refining the eight process changes proposed.

In the redesign stage, the group leader posted a message to the group with a description of the eight refined process changes agreed on by the group, the names of those responsible for implementing the changes, and the change implementation deadlines. No replies followed this posting.

Six out of eight process changes proposed by the group were implemented within six months of the group completion.

Results

A qualitative evaluation of the changes, based on departmental staff perceptions, indicated a slight increase in the perceived quality and productivity of the process redesigned, and a partial solution of the three main problems used as a starting point for the process improvement (PI) group discussion. The group leader perceived the outcome of the group discussion as positive and noted that the group discussion had allowed the department to tackle a number of problems that were long awaiting solution. For a number reasons, including busy individual timetables, these problems had not been dealt with for over six months prior to this PI group.

MAF.G2: The internal newsletter

Motivation

By the end of the facilitation of group MAF.G1, I was invited by the editor of MAF Quality Management's internal newsletter to facilitate a PI group expected to deal with three main problems:

- The lack of contributions to the newsletter.
- Recurring distortions, according to a number of newsletter contributor complaints, in the articles contributed by employees when they were finally published in the newsletter.
- Delays in the publication of several contributed articles, which in the past had led to the publication of outdated information.

All the above problems were perceived by the editor as being linked to the process of editing the newsletter. More specifically, the editor believed that the communication process between contributors and the newsletter's editor was at the source of most of those problems.

Formation

The newsletter's editor decided to lead the group. He invited four other members to take part in the group discussion. All of the invited members worked for the same division, a communications support division, and were based in different cities. Their day-to-day work was in different departments; they were involved only part-time in the process of editing the internal newsletter. Of the prospective group members, three, including the group leader, were in senior management or technical positions, and the other two were in assistant positions. All invited members agreed to participate in the discussion.

Features

The group lasted 26 days and, as indicated above, comprised five members from four departments in the same division. The members were based in four different cities. From the five agreeing to participate, only four members contributed postings to the discussion. The interaction in this group comprised nine electronic postings, and a number of one-on-one phone conversations.

According to estimates provided by group members, 89 percent of the total time spent by group members in the group discussion was in interactions through the EC system, whereas the remaining 11 percent was in oral one-on-one interactions.

Stages

In the definition stage, the group leader posted a message to the group containing a list with three problems and two processes, suggested as the main causes of the problems and thus as the target for the redesign. This posting was followed by three replies with comments on the leader's message, and whose content led to the selection of one process for redesign.

In the analysis stage, the leader posted a message to the group containing a textual description of the selected process split into eight activities, a summary with performance-related information, and three proposed changes. This posting was followed by one reply refining the process changes proposed.

In the redesign stage, the group leader posted a message to the group with a description of the three refined process changes agreed on by the group and the names of those responsible for implementing the changes right away. Two replies followed this posting agreeing with changes and praising the initiative.

All process changes proposed by the group were implemented within three months of the group completion.

Results

The newsletter editor perceived the group discussion as extremely useful, and said that he had the intention to conduct other similar PI groups in the future in his area. The problems that originated the group were reported by the editor as having been completely eliminated as a result of the process changes.

MAF.G3: Pest and disease outbreaks
Motivation

One of the key business processes performed by MAF Quality Management was that of media liaison during pest and disease outbreaks threatening New Zealand's agriculture. Such outbreaks had typically occurred no more than three times a year prior to this PI group.

During several outbreaks in the past, a main problem had been a lack of unified purpose and work coordination of the several teams reporting outbreaks to the media —mostly TV and radio stations, and newspapers. This had previously led to the release of misleading information to the public, as well as information that was not consistent for different parts of the country. Dealing with this problem was now a responsibility of a senior manager in the communications support division who had been a member of group MAF.G2.

Formation

The senior manager, motivated by his experience in group MAF.G2, requested me to facilitate a PI group led by him. He invited six other members to take part in the group discussion, all from the communications support division. Four of the invited members were senior managers or consultants; the other two were assistant consultants. The main background of all involved was, homogeneously, business communication. The invited members worked in offices located across five different cities, being only two of them, a senior and an assistant consultant, based on the same office and city. All invited members agreed to participate in the discussion.

Features

The group lasted 14 days and, as discussed above, comprised seven members from one department and six different cities. From the seven agreeing to participate, only three members contributed postings to the discussion. The interaction in this group comprised four electronic postings, a number of one-on-one phone and face-to-face conversations, and one group face-to-face meeting.

According to estimates provided by group members, 18 percent of the total time spent by group members in the group discussion was in interactions through the EC system, whereas the remaining 82 percent was in oral one-on-one or group interactions.

Stages

In the definition stage, the group leader posted a message to the group containing a list with three problems and two processes, suggested as the main causes of the problems and thus as the target for the redesign. This posting was followed by two replies with comments on the leader's message. This led to the selection of the two processes initially proposed by the leader for redesign.

The analysis stage was conducted through a one-day group meeting chaired by the leader, where seven process changes were discussed and refined by the group.

The redesign stage was conducted in the week after this meeting, where the group leader posted a message to the group with a description of the seven refined process changes agreed on by the group and the names of those responsible for implementing the changes right away. There were no replies to this posting. Four out of the seven proposed process changes were implemented within four months of the group completion.

The group leader, who was responsible for the coordination of the implementation of most of the process redesign proposals, left the organization before the next outbreak occurred.

Results

According to members of the communications support division the process changes led to a moderate increase in the quality and a reduction in the cost of the target processes. These improvements were reported when the communication team was brought into action again during a fruit-fly outbreak, approximately seven months after the PI group was completed.

MAF.G4: Quality management consulting
Motivation

Right after the group MAF.G3 was completed, I was introduced by MAF.G3's leader to a middle manager who had been assigned to solve a corporate-level problem. MAF Quality Management had a line of consulting products targeted at implementation of quality systems based on quality standards set by the government for the New Zealand food and plant industries.

MAF Quality Management's consulting products were tied to quality standards whose accreditation was the responsibility of a national accreditation body, which had recently launched a new standard aimed at small businesses. As a result of this launch, MAF Quality Management had to quickly develop a new consulting product tied to this new standard, and, in consequence, redesign some other consulting products to ensure product synergy. At the same time, MAF Quality Management had to avoid overlaps between this new product and other products already established in the market.

Formation

After a few meetings with me, where the group methodology was discussed, the middle manager decided to initiate a PI group discussion. He invited eight prospective group members. The invited members were from 4 different departments and based in five different cities. Two of the invited members were senior managers; the other six being in middle management or consulting positions.

Two main business backgrounds were evenly represented in the group, related to the main business areas at MAF Quality Management, namely "food" (mostly meat and dairy) and "plant." Unstructured interviews with employees prior to this group discussion suggested that each background was closely related to a specific business culture, being food personnel seen (by most of MAF Quality Management's employees with whom I talked to) as more aggressive and competitive. Food personnel were also seen as less polite than those who worked in the plant business, who were in turn typically seen as calm, cooperative, and polite.

All invited members agreed to participate in the discussion. Two other senior managers were included on request right after the PI discussion was begun.

The group leader decided to conduct the discussion in a less structured way than proposed by MetaProi, starting the group stages with more "subjective" postings and giving opportunity for members to, in his words, *"define the actual focus of the group"*.

I expressed concern about this lack of objectivity in the group discussion and the likely negative consequences, such as a possible lack of group focus. However, since I agreed to facilitate the group whatever the leader's decision might be, the group leader decided to carry on with his devised strategy at his own risk.

Features

The group lasted 30 days and, as discussed above, comprised 11 members from five departments and six different cities. From the 11 agreeing to participate, only seven members contributed postings to the discussion. The interaction in this group comprised 18 electronic postings and a number of one-on-one phone and face-to-face conversations.

According to estimates provided by group members, 80 percent of the total time spent by group members in the group discussion was in interactions through the EC system, whereas the remaining 20 percent was in oral one-on-one interactions.

Stages

In the definition stage, the group leader posted a message to the group defining the main problem to be tackled by the group in a very general and abstract way, and asking members to reply with the points they thought the group should focus on. This posting was followed by 9 replies with general and subjective comments on the main problem described, and raising new issues, some totally unrelated to the main problem posed to the group.

Noticing that the group discussion was lacking focus, the group leader posted a message summarizing previous postings and providing a more focused list of problems, related processes, and process changes. This posting was followed by 6 unfocused replies, one of which from a senior manager angrily criticizing the group's indecision.

Forecasting a likely lack of agreement and perhaps conflict in the group, the leader decided to discontinue the discussion. He did so by means of wrap-up posting calling for a face-to-face meeting to discuss whether the new quality standard should be adopted, and if yes, which changes in other consulting products should be implemented.

Results

No process changes were proposed. The group leader saw the group discussion as a failure. A month later the same set of issues tackled by this group were discussed in a different face-to-face group meeting, but again no agreement was achieved.

MAF.G5: Information technology support

Motivation

This group grew out of the need to target the process of providing information technology support to internal users as a whole, rather than only software users, as in group MAF.G1. In a sense, this group discussion was an extension of the discussion conducted by group MAF.G1.

Here, however, more general problems facing the information technology support team were targeted. Two other differences were that this group involved fewer information technology support employees in the group, being most of its members process customers, and that the person interested in leading this group was not a manager, but a senior computer support person. This person contacted me and asked me to facilitate the group discussion while group MAF.G4 was still being conducted.

Formation

The group leader invited 14 members to take part in the group discussion. Four of these members worked in the information technology department. One of them was the acting regional manager; the other 10 were process customers in senior and middle management, as well as technical non-management positions. The invited members were from six different departments, and were based in offices located in nine different cities. All those invited agreed to participate in the discussion.

Features

The group lasted 26 days and comprised 15 members from seven different departments spread through 10 different cities. From the 15 agreeing to participate, only 11 members contributed postings to the discussion. The interaction in this group comprised 23 electronic postings and a number of one-on-one phone and face-to-face conversations.

According to estimates provided by group members, 77 percent of the total time spent by group members in the group discussion was in interactions through the EC system, whereas the remaining 23 percent was in oral one-on-one interactions.

Stages

In the definition stage, the group leader posted a message to the group containing a list with four problems and five processes, suggested as the main causes of the problems and thus as the target for the redesign. This posting was followed by nine replies emphasizing some of the problems and proposing possible solutions. The analysis of these replies indicated an emphasis on two of the processes.

In the analysis stage, the leader posted a message to the group containing a textual description of the two selected processes, a summary with performance-related information, and a request for change proposals. This posting was followed by six replies proposing process changes, from which five were identified.

In the redesign stage, the group leader posted a message to the group with a description of the five process changes proposed by the group, the names of those responsible for implementing the changes, and implementation deadlines. Five replies followed this posting, refining the changes and praising the initiative.

Four out of five process changes were implemented within six months of the group completion.

Results

A survey of customer perceptions indicated an increase in perceived process quality. Perceptions of those who carried out activities in the process suggested an increase in the productivity of the process. During the implementation of the process changes, the leader of the information technology team was promoted to the position of regional manager of information technology support.

MAF.G6: Employee training and development

Motivation

This group arose from the need to improve the productivity and quality of the process of coordinating employee training and development. MAF Quality Management's large employee base had to be centrally and constantly monitored to ensure that employees would possess the skills and knowledge background needed in the projects they were routinely assigned to by their managers. These skills and knowledge background changed constantly. Among the change drivers were the introduction of new regulations or quality standards in the market, as illustrated by our description of group MAF.G4.

Monitoring and coordinating workers' qualifications and informing managers of the need for worker training was the responsibility of a multi-disciplinary team, which we shall call here "staff training coordination team." This team comprised members from several departments, and was facing a number of problems at the time I made contact with one of its members. Among the most pressing problems was the lack of a flexible and ease-to-use classification scheme for the description of employee qualifications embodying MAF Quality Management's constantly changing product portfolio.

Formation

During a chat with managers in the tea room, where I aired the intention to approach a possible leader for a sixth PI group to be facilitated at MAF Quality Management, I was told of some problems being faced by the staff training coordination team. Subsequently, I approached one of the senior members of this team and offered my services as a group facilitator.

After some meetings where the senior team member was briefed about MetaProi and the results of previous groups, he decided to lead a PI group and invited 13 other members to take part in the group discussion. The invited members were from 2 different departments and were based in 7 different cities. They worked in different departments, and were involved only part-time in the process of coordinating employee training and development. Of the prospective group members, about half were in senior management or technical positions; the other half held assistant positions. Assuming that most group members previously agreed that the key point to improve the target process was to develop a computer system, the prospective leader decided to use the group to define computer system requirements. All invited members agreed to participate in the discussion.

Features

The group lasted about 10 days as a PI group, being subsequently established as a semi-permanent forum for a discussion about software requirement specifications during approximately another three months. The group comprised 14 members from three departments and eight different cities. From the 14 agreeing to participate, only 6 members contributed postings to the discussion. The interaction in this group comprised six electronic postings and a number of one-on-one phone and face-to-face conversations.

According to estimates provided by group members 67 percent of the total time spent by group members in the group discussion was in interactions through the EC system, whereas the remaining 33 percent was in oral one-on-one interactions.

Stages

As mentioned earlier, the group leader started the group with the assumption that group members agreed that the key point to improve the already defined target process was to develop a computer system. Therefore, in the first message the leader tried to steer the group members into specifying the requirements of the computer system.

The group members reacted to this attempt by posting replies that were perceived by the group leader as "trivial," as well as suggesting lack of enthusiasm about the group discussion. After several phone and face-to-face contacts with group members, where they were asked to contribute more and better structured information, the leader grew increasing frustrated and finally decided to use the group discussion as a forum for permanent exchange of information about software requirements, rather than for process improvement. The goal of this forum was to complement face-to-face meetings.

Results

This group was seen as a failure by the group leader from a process improvement perspective. Moreover, three months after the PI group was discontinued, and the list server was defined as a forum to complement face-to-face computer system requirement specification meetings, I checked the list server and noticed that there had been no postings from group members. However, a further conversation with a member of the staff training coordination team suggested that the computer system requirement specification work was still under way, being most of the interaction carried out in face-to-face group meetings and one-on-one electronic messages between team members.

Waikato.G1: A practical computing course

Motivation

Waikato had recently set up a successful theoretical and practical computing course aimed at building student business computing skills on a number of software applications, including e-mail, group decision support systems, internet web browsers, word processors, spreadsheets, and database management systems.

While successful, with about 100 enrolments per semester, the course had recently been the focus of an avalanche of student complaints, which were perceived by management as negatively affecting Waikato's image. Most of the complaints were linked to the frequent computer problems experienced by students when trying to run their practical course assignments.

Formation

The person most directly involved with the practical component of the course was the course tutor, who was responsible for practical demonstrations in a computer laboratory during the time slots assigned for the course.

Both students and management had urged the course tutor to come up with innovative solutions to reduce or eliminate computer problems experienced by students. His first step was to bring together members of the two departments directly involved in the practical component of the course, a computer support and an academic department.

Those members were initially reluctant to meet and discuss those problems because of previous conflicts between the two departments, who blamed each other for the problems in the course. However, they eventually agreed to participate in the PI group led by the course tutor when they knew that the discussion would take place through an EC system. Computer mediation was perceived by most of them as likely to lead to a less formal and less confrontational discussion, differently from what would likely happen in face-to-face meetings.

Features

The PI group lasted 33 days and comprised 7 members from both the computer support and the academic departments. The interaction in the group comprised 21 postings, and a number of one-on-one phone and face-to-face conversations.

According to estimates provided by group members, 71 percent of the total time spent by group members in the group discussion was in interactions through the EC system, whereas the remaining 29 percent was in oral one-on-one interactions.

Stages

In the definition stage, the group leader posted a message to the group containing a list with eight problems and three processes, suggested as the main causes of the problems and thus as the target for redesign. This posting was followed by 4 replies with comments on the leader's message, whose content led to the selection of 2 processes for redesign.

In the analysis stage, the leader posted a message to the group containing a flow chart description of the 2 selected processes (as a file attached to the message), a summary with performance-related information, and six proposed changes. This posting was followed by 13 replies, and the group agreed on five process changes.

In the redesign stage, the group leader posted a message to the group with a description of the five process changes agreed on by the group, the names of those responsible for implementing the changes, and change implementation deadlines.

Results

The group was completed in time for change implementation and impact assessment during the following course semester. All changes were implemented either before or during the course semester, and their impact was assessed through a survey on student perceptions about the course. The survey indicated a remarkable improvement in the quality of the course, when compared with a previous survey performed in the previous semester, and covered most of the points targeted by the PI group.

Waikato.G2: Academic advice for students

Motivation

The general problem that this group wanted to discuss was the increasing level of litigation brought against Waikato by students, with regard to the academic and program advice they received from staff and faculty members. More specifically, this general problem included issues such as:

- Increased instances of litigation by students having made significant academic program decisions based on incorrect advice.
- Increased instances of the head of the organization having to use his special (regulatory) powers to waive regulations due to litigation.
- Faculty members having differing expectations of administrative staff with regard to whom should give what advice to students.

Formation

The self-appointed group leader was a senior administrative staff who reported directly to the head of one of the Waikato's business units. This particular business unit was chosen because it was at the source of most of the student litigation problems in the previous year.

A number of people were invited and agreed to contribute to the PI group. Two of them were intermediate administrative staff, and one was a senior administrative staff who had previously been involved in strategy-focused discussions about this issue. Two among the other invited people were faculty members, and, finally, two others were heads of academic departments.

Features

This PI group lasted 41 days and involved five departments, represented by the eight members just mentioned. All of the eight members who agreed to participate in the group contributed postings to the discussion. The interaction comprised 30 postings and a small number of one-on-one telephone and face-to-face conversations.

According to estimates provided by the group members, 96 percent of the total discussion time spent by group members was in interactions through the EC system; four percent of the time was in oral one-on-one interactions.

Stages

In the definition stage of the discussion, the leader posted a message that detailed four problems and two potential process causes. Initially two causes were proposed: (a) that there was a lack of training on the part of key faculty and general staff members; and (b) that students did not have immediate access to faculty members, and therefore should seek the advice of administrative staff members. Thirteen replies followed this initial message commenting on the group leader and others' postings, and proposing change suggestions focused on two business processes.

In the analysis stage, these two processes were described and two proposals for process change were made. This message elicited five responses, which modified the tentative change proposals. Unfortunately, at this stage, some information had been missing from the discussion because of the confidential nature of the litigation issue. However one of the departmental heads had candidly contributed potential issues from his own department which in some way alleviated that particular gap in the discussion material.

Finally, in the redesign stage, two changes were proposed, consolidating previous change proposals. This posting was followed by nine replies commenting on the changes and proposing minor amendments. While one of these change proposals received almost unanimous support from the group, the other was only partially supported.

Results

Although a time line and responsibilities were set for the implementation of the two process changes resulting from this group, these changes were never actually implemented. It was later found that one of the members assigned responsibility for implementing the process changes was not committed to the change process. This person perceived the discussion as lacking, in her own words, "legitimacy and authority".

Waikato.G3: Student computer support

Motivation

Some time after Waikato.G2 had been completed, and shortly before new computing facilities were to be made available, a discussion was initiated to improve the entire student computing experience at one of Waikato's computer facilities. It housed 150 computers and seven printers. Soon a new area would be made available, adding 75 new machines.

Although the computer system and support staff had been able to accommodate teaching requirements, providing computer support to students was generally seen as a troublesome task. Many problems were caused by changes to courses by academic departments that were not effectively communicated to computer support staff. Alternately, changes to the computer system that alleviated previous problems or caused new ones were not being communicated back to faculty members. Professors needed this feedback in order to change course material. These problems were similar to those found in Waikato.G1.

Formation

A course tutor, who had also been a student at the institution, led the PI discussion. He had worked in the computer facility in a user support role, and was familiar with the concept of PI. The manager of the computer facility was eager to obtain some strategic input from outside of his immediate support staff. The leader convinced computer support staff and senior members of 5 teaching units, who had computer related material in their course curricula, to become members of the PI group.

Features

The PI group lasted 32 days and involved 11 members from five departments. From the 11 agreeing to participate, only seven members contributed postings to the discussion. The interaction in the group comprised 23 postings, as well as some one-on-one oral (mostly face-to-face) conversations.

According to estimates provided by the group members, 81 percent of the total time spent by group members in the group discussion was in interactions through the EC system; the other 19 percent in oral one-on-one interactions.

Stages

In the definition stage, the leader posted a message to the group containing a list with five problems, phrased as generic areas of complaint by students, and four processes to be targeted for redesign. This posting was followed by four replies developing two distinct themes. The first theme was that some faculty members considered complaints from the students as being outside of their area of responsibility. The second theme was that workable solutions did indeed exist, and several members offered a variety of these.

At this point, the leader tried to force the discussion onto the processes proposed by him through a message posted to the group. This was done in an attempt to both focus the discussion and create a climate for the development of appropriate solutions. This message, however, was largely ignored in the six replies that followed.

In spite of this, the leader proceeded to the analysis stage with a posting in which he described one of the processes (split into 10 main activities) by means of a non-standard diagram attached to the posting, and a list with 3 proposed changes. This was followed by five replies, again, totally unrelated to the leader's posting.

A "harsh" posting from the leader aimed at redirecting the discussion was rebutted in a reply from one of the members, a senior lecturer. At this point, the leader, upon advice from the facilitator, posted a message to the group apologizing for his "harsh tone" in the previous posting. This was followed by a reply that was again totally unrelated to the main topic of the discussion.

A concluding message by the leader highlighted the major themes of the discussion and concluded that the computer support staff were the best people to decide their own fate. No replies followed.

Results

Although this conclusion was negative in PI terms, as the group failed to generate any process improvement proposal, group members were generally pleased with the discussion itself. Some members noted that the discussion had promoted dissemination of interdepartmental knowledge, while others, notably computer support staff, saw the group discussion as an endorsement of their good work.

Waikato.G4: Student assignments

Motivation

The amount of course-related data exchanged between faculty and students has led to the creation of support departments whose common characteristic was to coordinate the handling of these data from and to teachers and students of several departments. Such departments were typically within a school of studies.

For the sake of this group's description, I shall generically refer to these support departments as student handout places or SHOPs. Course-related data flowing from teachers to students in SHOPs typically involved course assignment instructions, course readings, marked assignments, and documentation about external organizations; the latter typically used in courses with fieldwork content. Course-related data flowing from students to faculty in SHOPs typically involved completed assignment forms.

This PI group emerged out of the interest of a SHOP manager, who had recently arrived at Waikato, in turning the process of handling student assignments into a more efficient one.

Formation

I met the SHOP manager informally at a tearoom, while talking to the leader of a previous group, and after being told about the manager's ideas about possible improvements in the SHOP, offered to facilitate a PI group led by the SHOP manager. She decided to invite three faculty members, two students, and one administrative staff to participate in the group discussion.

Features

The group lasted 45 days and involved seven members from five departments. From the seven members who agreed to participate, only five contributed postings to the discussion. The interaction in the group comprised 15 postings and some one-on-one oral (mostly face-to-face) conversations.

According to estimates provided by the group members, 77 percent of the total time spent by group members in the group discussion was in interactions through the EC system; the other 23 percent being in oral one-on-one interactions.

Stages

In the definition stage, the leader posted a message to the group containing a list with five problems and five processes, presented as the possible sources of the problems. This posting was followed by 9 replies focusing on two of the processes listed. These processes related the actual handling of course material, and the way communication between faculty members and SHOP staff was conducted regarding course assignment handling issues.

In the analysis stage, the group leader posted a message to the group summarizing contributions and providing a textual description of two processes. In this message she also summarized some qualitative information about the performance of the processes, and promise to look up some extra technical information to be summarized in a future posting. She also proposed 4 process changes. Two replies followed this posting with general comments, one of them questioning the completeness and correctness of the process descriptions.

Ignoring this criticism, the group leader then posted a message summarizing some technical issues related to the implementation of the process changes, which pointed to the implementation of 2 changes relating the setting up of three items. The first was a new computerized bar-coding system for keeping track of course material. The second item were Internet web pages with standard cover sheets for the assignments. The third were bar-codes for the students.

This was followed by one final wrap-up posting from the group leader summarizing two proposed process changes, responsibilities and implementation deadlines. The main responsibility for the coordination of the implementation of the two process changes lay on the group leader.

Both of the process changes were partially implemented in pilot projects within three months of the group completion, and their full implementation was scheduled to be conducted within the next six months. One posting from the leader followed shortly after with some more details about process-change implementation issues. No replies followed.

Results

An assessment of the pilot projects, which involved faculty members and SHOP staff, as well as over 150 students, indicated a drastic increase in process productivity and a moderate increase in the quality of the process. The computerized bar-coding system in particular, was seen by the SHOP's manager, as well as some teachers, as likely to allow SHOP staff to move from predominantly manual and "mechanical" activities towards knowledge-intensive roles. Examples of the latter were providing support to students and academics as to where and how to find relevant information for research and courses.

Waikato.G5: International graduate students

Motivation

Waikato's support structure to international students comprised a central international student's office plus a number of decentralized departments within schools of studies. One major problem facing one of these decentralized departments, known at Waikato as international student departments, was that permanent resident students were not required to meet the same English standards as international students did. Permanent resident students were those who had been born outside New Zealand and had legally migrated to the country.

International students had to fulfill a number of requirements, including a minimum score in the TOEFL test (Test of English as a Foreign Language), before they could enroll in any course. While the international students office was prepared to cater for the needs of these students, it did not have the resources to provide support for permanent resident students whose, for example, English language skills were way bellow those of entry-level international students. As permanent resident students received the same treatment as New Zealand nationals, they were not considered in budget allocation decisions regarding the international student department. Nevertheless, a number of these students were routinely asked by their lecturers to seek support from the international student department. The reason was because, as one of the lecturers put it, "...*they [i.e. the permanent resident students] look like international students...*" In fact, most international students in New Zealand, as well as immigrants in general, were from Asian countries. They were thus indiscriminately seen as members of the same group, as far as academic issues were concerned. Most lecturers, typically from European or North-American backgrounds, saw these students as simply "international students".

Formation

I was advised to contact the international student's department manager by one of Waikato's senior professors who had been facing difficulties in dealing with permanent resident students. When approached, this manager told me that she had asked for a budget increase so she could also cater for the needs of permanent resident students. She wanted to embrace this responsibility, however problematic it might me, because, in her words, "...*if we don't do it, the competition will...*" Moreover, Waikato had recently tried to build up an image of a multi-cultural institution, and this was an opportunity for Waikato to reaffirm its commitment.

On the other hand, the manager declared having experienced some difficulties in the past with her superiors because of her ideas. Among other things, they seemed determined to postpone any decision regarding differential treatment to permanent resident students. She saw the PI group as a last resort to resolve the permanent resident students issue, and decided to invite a broad range of members to take part in the group. Among these were some of her superiors and faculty members, as well as international and permanent resident students.

Features

The group lasted 33 days and involved 13 members from 8 departments. From the 13 agreeing to participate, only 8 members contributed postings to the discussion. Three out of the five members who contributed no electronic postings to the discussion actively participated in a face-to-face group discussion conducted in the analysis stage of the group. The interaction in the group comprised 22 postings, a number of one-on-one e-mail messages, some one-on-one oral conversations, and one group face-to-face meeting.

According to estimates provided by the group members, 52 percent of the total time spent by group members in the group discussion was in interactions through the EC system; the other 48 percent being in oral interactions.

Stages

In the definition stage, the leader posted a message to the group containing a list with four problems and three processes, presented as the possible sources of the problems. These processes related the way:

- Support was provided to students with English problems.
- Communication between the department and students was conducted.
- Students were matched with supervisors.

This posting was followed by six replies, one of these correcting the description of some of the problems and expanding the scope of one of the processes presented. The other five postings provided general and vague comments on some of the issues raised in the first message.

At this point the group leader was summoned to a meeting with her superiors and was advised to discontinue the PI group discussion. Although the manager refused to discuss all the content of this meeting with me, it became apparent that her superiors saw the conduct of the discussion through the EC system as inappropriate, as the discussion could trigger comments about racial issues. They feared that discussion transcripts could later be used against Waikato in formal complaints and perhaps law suits by students from ethnic minorities.

As a result, the manager decided to shift the focus of the group discussion towards a related and less politically sensitive issue— the nature of the support provided to international graduate students. She tried to do this in a posting where she explained to the group that the change in the focus of the group was due to a low response rate. She subsequently described five main problems. She also described 1 process, which was presented as the source of the problems.

The reason why the manager decided not to tell the group the real reason for the shift in the focus of the group was that her superiors requested that their previous meeting be kept secret. This posting was followed by 12 replies. Only five of them were related to the new discussion topic. The remaining seven postings were related to the old topic—permanent resident students support. These postings suggested some unease about the sudden change of topic.

Given the seeming perplexity of some group members, a face-to-face meeting was then called by the group leader to conduct the next stage of the group discussion. Six group members attended the face-to-face meeting, which lasted approximately 2 hours and 15 minutes. In this face-to-face meeting, the group leader stuck to the new topic. She supplied the group with a process description and performance-related information, and proposed four process changes for discussion.

The group agreed on three process changes, which, together with the information supplied, were summarized in a posting from the group leader to the group, a few days after the face-to-face meeting. One reply followed acknowledging this posting.

The group leader left Waikato right after the group was completed, being her successor responsible for coordinating the implementation of the process changes agreed on by the group.

Three months after the group completion one of the process changes had been fully implemented and the other two had been partially implemented.

Results

An unstructured interview with the new international student's support department manager, conducted approximately three months after the group completion, indicated satisfaction with the outcome of the process change implementation. It had, in her view, led to a moderate improvement in the quality of the services provided by her department. Unstructured interviews with a few international graduate students confirmed this perception.

Waikato.G6: New international students

Motivation

Approximately 8 months before this PI group was begun a system whereby senior students helped newly arrived international students with their cultural and educational adaptation was set in place by the international students office, mentioned in Waikato.G5, which had now been renamed "international office". This system was called the *buddy system* and was based on the idea that local senior students can pass on their experience in dealing with life at Waikato and social life matters in general to international students, and, at the same time, get a valuable input from other cultures.

The buddy system involved both New Zealand and senior international students who helped newly arrived international students. At the *buddy system*, which was seen as a type of "club," the local mentors were called *local buddies* and the newly arrived international students were called *international buddies*.

There were some problems with this system, which were seen as needing urgent attention since the *buddy system* was perceived by some of Waikato's top managers as having the potential to give the institution an "edge" over other universities in the Australasian region.

One of the problems was that there were not enough local buddies (only 6 by the time this PI group started). In addition, participation of native New Zealand students in the buddy system was low. A number of the local students assigned to the buddy system had the same cultural background, and in some cases, spoke the same native language as the new international students. Although this was seen as likely to reduce the initial "cultural shock" experienced by international buddies, it was often seen by international buddies themselves as an obstacle for them to have a deeper contact with a truly different culture and to improve their English skills. Finally there was a perceived lack of initiative from local buddies to identify and meet the needs of the international buddies, who, in turn, often did not know how to approach and get help from their local buddies.

Formation

This group was a result of a request made to me by one of the members of the international office mentioned in Waikato.G5 who had participated in that group as a member. This prospective leader had recently been assigned a middle management position in his office, and one of his responsibilities was, in his words: "... *to make the buddy system work* ..."

This ex-member wanted to lead, with my facilitation, a PI group in the mid-semester break to improve the process involved in providing support to new international students through the buddy system. He decided to invite the director of his area, his manager, local buddies, and international buddies to participate in the

PI group discussion. By doing so, he expected to have a wide range of opinions represented in the group discussion, and bring the "voice" of the customers (i.e. the international buddies) of the process into the discussion.

Features

The group lasted 54 days and involved 11 members from 4 departments (student departments were considered those were the students were doing their majors). From the 11 members who agreed to participate, only seven contributed postings to the discussion. The interaction in the group comprised 15 postings, a number of one-on-one e-mail messages, some one-on-one oral conversations, and one group face-to-face meeting. The group face-to-face meeting was conducted as part of the analysis stage. It lasted approximately two hours and involved only five members who had previously contributed postings.

According to estimates provided by the group members, 75 percent of the total time spent by them in the group discussion was in interactions through the EC system; the other 35 percent in oral interactions.

Stages

In the definition stage, the leader posted a message to the group containing a list with six problems and four processes, presented as the possible sources of the problems. These processes related local buddy selection criteria, guidelines to be followed by these students when dealing with international buddies, and the communication between international office staff, local buddies, and international buddies.

The leader's initial posting was followed by 11 replies showing strong agreement about the lack of enough effective communication channels between local and international buddies. A number of these postings already included suggestions on how to improve this situation. A posting from the group leader summarized these contributions and started the analysis stage. In this posting, the group leader described the general process of providing support to international buddies by discussing several characteristics of the buddy system, rather than following the workflow format suggested in MetaProi's guide. He proposed three main changes for this general process. His posting was followed by only 1 reply praising the initiative and emphasizing the need for more efficient and effective communication channels between local and international buddies.

The lack of more participation prompted the leader to contact PI group members, both over the phone and face-to-face, and invite them to take part in a face-to-face group meeting. This meeting was eventually conducted with only five of the PI group members who agreed to participate. It lasted, as mentioned before, approximately two hours. In this meeting, PI group members agreed on four process changes, which were summarized in a posting from the group leader to the group a few days after. No replies followed.

Three months after the group completion, all process changes were in the process of being implemented. Two of those changes had been almost fully implemented by then.

Results

One unstructured interview and a number of informal conversations with the new international student's support department manager, conducted approximately three months after the group completion, indicated satisfaction with the outcome of the process change implementation. In her view, it led to a moderate improvement in the quality of the general process targeted. Unstructured interviews with a few international buddies confirmed this perception.

Bibliography

Alster, N. (1997), Do US Firms Spend Too Much on Information Technology?, *Investor's Business Daily*, April 3.

Argyris, C. (1977), Double Loop Learning Organizations, *Harvard Business Review*, September-October.

Argyris, C. (1992), *On Organizational Learning*, Blackwell, Cambridge, MA.

Argyris, C. and Schon, D. (1978), *Organizational Learning: A Theory of Action Perspective*, Addison-Wesley, Reading, MA.

Bannon, L.J. (1993), CSCW: An Initial Exploration, *Scandinavian Journal of Information Systems*, V.5.

Bartlett, F.C. (1932), *Remembering*, Cambridge University Press, Cambridge, MA.

Boland Jr., R.J. and Tenkasi, R.V. (1995), Perspective Making and Perspective Taking in Communities of Knowing, *Organization Science*, V.6, No.4.

Boroson, W. (1997), *Keys to Investing in Mutual Funds*, Barron's Educational Series, Hauppauge, NY.

Budd, J.M. and Raber, D. (1996), Discourse Analysis: Method and Application in the Study of Information, *Information Processing & Management*, V.32, No.2.

Caldwell, B. (1994), Missteps, Miscues, *InformationWEEK*, June 20.

Callatay, A.M. (1986), *Natural and Artifical Intelligence*, North-Holland, Amsterdam, The Netherlands.

Camèrer, C.F. and Johnson, E.J. (1991), The Process-Performance Paradox in Expert Judgment, *Toward a General Theory of Expertise*, Ericsson, K.A. and Smith, J. (Eds), Cambridge University Press, Cambridge, MA.

Caron, J.R., Jarvenpaa, S.L., and Stoddard, D.B. (1994), Business Reengineering at CIGNA Corporation: Experiences and Lessons Learned From the First Five Years, *MIS Quarterly*, V.18, No.3.

Champy, J. (1995), *Reengineering Management,* Harper Business, New York, NY.

CHE (1995), The Learning Organization, *Chief Executive*, March.

Checkland, P. (1981), *Systems Thinking, Systems Practice*, John Wiley & Sons, New York, NY.

Checkland, P. and Scholes, J. (1990), *Soft Systems Methodology in Action*, John Wiley & Sons, New York, NY.

Childe, S.J., Maull, R.S. and Benett, J. (1994), Frameworks for Understanding Business Process Re-engineering, *International Journal of Operations & Productions Management,* V.14, No.12.

Childe, S.J. (1995), Business Process Re-engineering, *Management Bibliographies & Reviews*, V.21, No.3.

Choi, T.Y. and Behling, O.C. (1997), Top Managers and TQM Success: One More Look After all These Years, *The Academy of Management Executive*, V.11, No.1.

Crosby, P.B. (1980), *Quality is Free: The Art of Making Quality Certain*, Mentor, New York, NY.

Crosby, P.B. (1984), *Quality without Tears: The Art of Hassle-free Management*, McGraw-Hill, New York, NY.

Daft, R.L. and Lengel, R.H. (1986), Organizational Information Requirements, Media Richness and Structural Design, *Management Science*, V.32, No.5.

Daft, R.L., Lengel, R.H. and Trevino, L.K. (1987), Message Equivocality, Media Selection, and Manager Performance: Implications for Information Systems, *MIS Quarterly*, V.11, No.3.

Davenport, T.H. (1993), *Process Innovation*, Harvard Business Press, Boston, MA.

Davenport T.H. (1993a), Need Radical Innovation and Continuous Improvement? Integrate Process Re-engineering and Total Quality Management, *Planning Review*, V.21, No.3.

Davenport, T.H., Jarvenpaa, S.L. and Beers, M.C. (1996), Improving Knowledge Work Processes, *Sloan Management Review*, V.37, No.4.

Davenport, T.H. and Short, J.E. (1990), The New Industrial Engineering: Information Technology and Business Process Redesign, *Sloan Management Review*, Summer.

Davenport, T.H. and Stoddard, D.B. (1994), Reengineering: Business Change of Mythic Proportions?, *MIS Quarterly*, V.18, No.2.

Davidow, W.H. and Malone, M.S. (1992), *The Virtual Corporation*, HarperCollins, New York, NY.

Davis, W.S. (1983), *System Analysis and Design: A Structured Approach*, Addison-Wesley, Reading, MA.

DeMarco, T. (1979), Structured Analysis and System Specification, Prentice-Hall, Englewood Cliffs, N.J.

Deming, W.E. (1986), *Out of The Crisis*, MIT, Center for Advanced Engineering Study, Cambridge, MA.

Dennett, D.C. (1991), *Consciousness Explained*, Little, Brown and Co., Boston, MA.

Dennis, A.R., Haley, B.J. and Vanderberg, R.J. (1996), A Meta-analysis of Effectiveness, Efficiency, and Participant Satisfaction in Group Support Systems Research, *Proceedings of the 17th International Conference on Information Systems*, DeGross, J.I., Jarvenpaa, S. and Srinivasan, A. (Eds), The Association for Computing Machinery, New York, NY.

Dingle, M.E. (1994), *Business Process Reengineering: A New Zealand Perspective*, Research Report, Department of Executive Education, Massey University, Palmerston North, New Zealand.

Dozier, R.W., Jr. (1992), *Codes of Evolution*, Crown Publishers, New York, NY.

Drucker, P.F. (1989), *The New Realities*, Harper & Row, New York, NY.

Drucker, P.F. (1995), Rethinking Work, *Executive Excellence*, February.

Eason, K. (1996), Division of Labour and the Design of Systems for Computer Support for Cooperative Work, *Journal of Information Technology*, V.11, No.1.

Feldman, J. (1986), On the Difficulty of Learning from Experience, *The Thinking Organization*, Sims, H.P., Jr. and Gioia, D.A. (Eds), Jossey-Bass, San Francisco, CA.

Galbraith, J.K. (1973), *Designing Complex Organizations*, Addison-Wesley, Reading, MA.

Gane, C. and Sarson, T. (1979), *Structured Systems Analysis: Tools and Techniques*,

Prentice-Hall, Englewood Cliffs, N.J.

Gardner, H. (1985), *The Mind's New Science*, Basic Books, New York, NY.

Garratt, R. (1994), *The Learning Organization*, HarperCollins, London, UK.

Geyelin, M. (1994), Doomsday Device, *The Wall Street Journal*, August 8.

Gleick, J. (1993), *Chaos: Making a New Science*, Abacus, London, UK.

Gore, M. and Stubbe, J.W. (1988), *Elements of Systems Analysis*, Brown Publishers, Dubuque, IA.

Goldratt, E.M. (1991), *The Haystack Syndrome: Sifting Information Out of the Data Ocean*, North River Press, New York, NY.

Goldratt, E.M. and Fox, R.E. (1986), *The Race*, North River Press, New York, NY.

Grudin, J. (1994), Groupware and Social Dynamics: Eight Challenges for Developers, *Communications of the ACM*, V.37, No.1.

Grudin, J. (1994a), CSCW: History and Focus, *IEEE Computer*, V.27, No.5.

Guha, S., Kettinger, W.J. and Teng, J.T.C. (1993), Business Process Reengineering, Building a Comprehensive Methodology, *Information Systems Management*, Summer.

Hackett, P. (1990), Investment in Technology-The Service Sector Sinkhole?, *Sloan Management Review*, Winter.

Hall, G., Rosenthal, J. and Wade, J. (1993), How to Make Reengineering Really Work, *Harvard Business Review*, November-December.

Hammer, M. (1990), Reengineering Work: Don't Automate, Obliterate, *Harvard Business Review*, July-August.

Hammer, M.E. (1996), *Beyond Reengineering*, HarperCollins, New York, NY.

Hammer, M. and Champy, J. (1993), *Reengineering the Corporation*, Harper Business, New York, NY.

Hammer, M. and Stanton, S.A. (1995), *The Reengineering Revolution*, HarperCollins, New York, NY.

Harrington, H.J. (1991), *Business Process Improvement*, McGraw-Hill, New York, NY.

Hawking, S.W. (1988), *A Brief History of Time*, Bantam Books, New York, NY.

Hayek, F.A. (1996), The Use of Knowledge in Society, *Knowledge Management and Organizational Design*, Myers, P.S. (Ed), Butterworth-Heinemann, Boston, MA.

Hendricks, K.B. and Singhal, V.R. (1997), Does Implementing an Effective TQM Program Actually Improve Operating Performance? Empirical Evidence from Firms that Have Won Quality Awards, *Management Science*, V.43, No.9.

Hirschheim, R.A. (1985), *Office Automation: A Social and Organizational Perspective*, John Wiley & Sons, New York, NY.

Holsapple, C.W. and Whinston, A.B. (1996), *Decision Support Systems: A Knowledge-Based Approach*, West Publishing, St. Paul, MN.

Holyoak, K.J. (1991), Symbolic Connectionism: Toward Third-Generation Theories of Expertise, *Toward a General Theory of Expertise*, Ericsson, K.A. and Smith, J. (Eds), Cambridge University Press, Cambridge, MA.

Hunt, V.D. (1996), *Process Mapping: How to Reengineer your Business Processes*, John Wiley & Sons, New York, NY.

Ishikawa, K. (1986). *Guide to Quality Control*, Asian Productivity Organization, Tokyo, Japan.

Jacobson, I., Ericsson, M. and Jacobson, A. (1995), *The Object Advantage*, Addison-

Wesley, New York, NY.

Jessup, L.M. and Tansik, D.A. (1991), Decision Making in an Automated Environment: The Effects of Anonymity and Proximity with a Group Decision Support System, *Decision Sciences*, V.22, No.2.

Juran, J. (1989), *Juran on Leadership for Quality*, The Free Press, New York, NY.

Katzenbach, J.R. and Smith, D.K. (1993), *The Wisdom of Teams: Creating the High-performance Organization*, Harvard Business School Press, Boston, MA.

Kock, N. (1995), *MetaProi: A Group Process for Business Process Improvement*, Project Report GP-G-1995-R5, Dept. of Management Systems, University of Waikato, Hamilton, New Zealand.

Kock, N. (1995a), *Process Reengineering, PROI: A Practical Methodology*, Editora Vozes, Sao Paulo, Brazil (in Portuguese).

Kock, N.(1997), Fostering Interdepartmental Knowledge Communication Through Groupware: A Process Improvement Perspective, *Proceedings of the International Conference on Supporting Group Work*, Hayne, S.C. and Prinz, W. (Eds), The Association for Computing Machinery, New York, NY.

Kock, N. and Corner, J.L. (1997), Improving University Processes through Computer-Mediated Process Redesign Groups, *Campus-Wide Information Systems*, V.14, No.1.

Kock Jr., N. and McQueen, R.J. (1995), Integrating Groupware Technology into a Business Process Improvement Framework, *Information Technology & People*, V.8, No.4.

Kock, N. and McQueen, R.J. (1996), Product Flow, Breadth and Complexity of Business Processes: An Empirical Study of Fifteen Business Processes in Three Organizations, *Business Process Re-engineering & Management*, V.2, No.2.

Kock, N. and McQueen, R.J. (1997), Using Groupware in Quality Management Programs, *Information Systems Management*, V.14, No.2.

Kock, N. and McQueen, R.J. (1998), An Action Research Study of Effects of Asynchronous Groupware Support on Productivity and Outcome Quality of Process Redesign Groups, *Journal of Organizational Computing and Electronic Commerce*, V.8, No.2.

Kock, N.F., McQueen, R.J. and Baker, M. (1996), Learning and Process Improvement in Knowledge Organizations: A Critical Analysis of Four Contemporary Myths, *The Learning Organization*, V.3, No.1.

Kock, N., McQueen, R.J. and Corner, J.L. (1997), The Nature of Data, Information and Knowledge Exchanges in Business Processes: Implications for Process Improvement and Organizational Learning, *The Learning Organization*, V.4, No.2.

Kock, N. and Tomelin, C.A. (1996), *PMQP: Total Quality Management in Practice*, Business Development Center, SENAC, Curitiba, Brazil (in Portuguese).

Kofman, F. and Senge, P.M. (1993), The Heart of Learning Organizations, *Organization Dynamics*, V.22, No.2,

Kogut, B. and Zander, U. (1992), Knowledge of the Firm, Combinative Capabilities, and the Replication of Technology, *Organization Science*, V.3, No.3.

Kryt, J. (1997), Information Conundrum: Semantics...With a Payoff!, *Informatica*, V.21, No.2.

Kurke, L.B. and Aldrich, H.E. (1983), Mintzberg was Right!: A Replication and

Extension of the Nature of Managerial Work, *Management Science*, V.29, No.8.

Lee, A.S. (1994), Electronic Mail as a Medium for Rich Communication: An Empirical Investigation Using Hermeneutic Interpretation, *MIS Quarterly*, V.18, No.2.

Lengel, R.H. and Daft, R.L. (1988), The Selection of Communication Media as an Executive Skill, *Academy of Management Executive*, V.2, No.3.

Lewin, R. (1993), An Orderly Progression out of Chaos, *New Scientist*, June 5.

Lord, R.G. and Foti, R.J. (1986), Schema Theories, Information Processing and Organizational Behaviour, *The Thinking Organization*, Sims, H.P., Jr. and Gioia, D.A. (Eds), Jossey-Bass, San Francisco, CA.

Malone, T.W. and Crowston, K. (1994), The Interdisciplinaly Study of Coordination, *ACM Computing Surveys*, V.26, No.1.

Mark, J.A. (1984), Productivity Measurement: The Government's Role in the United States, *The Measurement and Implications of Productivity Growth*, Sherer, P. and Malone, T. (Eds), Australian Government Publishing Service, Canberra, Australia.

Martin, J. (1991), *Rapid Application Development*, Macmillan, New York, NY.

Maull, R., S. Childe, J. Bennett, A.M Weaver, and P.A. Smart (1995), *Report on Different Types of Manufacturing Processes and IDEF0 Models Describing Standard Business Processes*, Working Paper WP/GR/J95010-4, School of Computing, University of Plymouth, Plymouth, England.

Meyer, B. (1998), The Future of Object Technology, *IEEE Computer*, V.31, No.1.

Miller, G.A. (1956), The Magical Number Seven, Plus or Minus Two: Some Limits on Our Capacity for Processing Information, *The Psychological Review*, V.63.

Mintzberg, H. (1975), The Manager's Job: Folklore and Fact, *Harvard Business Review*, July-August.

Misterek, S.D.A., Dooley, K.J. and Anderson, J.C. (1992), Productivity as a Performance Measure, *International Journal of Operations & Production Management*, V. 12, No. 1.

Mowshowitz, A. (1997), Virtual Organization, *Communications of the ACM*, V.40, No.9.

Nelson, K.M. and Cooprider, J.G. (1996), The Contribution of Shared Knowledge to IS Group Performance, *MIS Quarterly*, V.20, No.4.

Nevis, E.C., DiBella, A.J. and Gould, J.M. (1995), Understanding Organisations as Learning Systems, *Sloan Management Review*, Winter.

Nosek, J. and McNeese, M.D. (1997), Issues for Knowledge Management from Experiences in Supporting Group Knowledge Elicitation and Creation in Ill-Defined, Emerging Situations, *Proceedings of the AIII Spring Symposium on Artificial Intelligence in Knowledge Management*, Gaines, B.R. (Ed), Department of Computer Science, The University of Calgary, Alberta, Canada.

Olson, D.L. and Courtney, J.F., Jr. (1992), *Decision Support Models and Expert Systems*, Macmillan, New York, NY.

Orlikowski, W.J. (1992), Learning from Notes: Organizational Issues in Groupware Implementation, *Proceedings of CSCW'92 Conference*, Turner, J. and Kraut, R. (Eds), The Association for Computing Machinery, New York, NY.

Ould, M.A. (1995), *Business Processes: Modelling and Analysis for Re-engineering and Improvement*, John Wiley & Sons, Chichester, England.

Partridge, C. (1994), Modelling the Real World: Are Classes Abstractions or Objects?, *Journal of Object-Oriented Programming*, V.7, No.7.

Peters, T.J. and Waterman, R.H., Jr. (1982), *In Search of Excellence*, Harper & Row, New York, NY.

Pinker, S. (1997), *How the Mind Works*, W.W. Norton & Co., New York, NY.

Porter, M.E. (1980), *Competitive Strategy: Techniques for Analyzing Industries and Competitors*, The Free Press, New York, NY.

Porter, M.E. (1985), *Competitive Advantage*, The Free Press, New York, NY.

Prahalad, C.K. and Hamel, G.K. (1990), The Core Competence of the Corporation, *Harvard Business Review*, V.68, No.3.

Pressman, R. (1987), *Software Engineering: A Practitioner's Approach*, McGraw-Hill, New York, NY.

Probst, G.J.B. and Buchel, B.S.T. (1997), *Organizational Learning: The Competitive Advantage of the Future*, Prentice Hall, London, England.

Ramsey, D.K. (1987), *The Corporate Warriors*, Houghton Mifflin, Boston, MA.

Redding, J.C. and Catalanello, R.F. (1994), *Strategic Readiness: The Making of the Learning Organization*, Jossey-Bass, San Francisco, CA.

Rogers, Y. (1992), Ghosts in the Network: Distributed Troubleshooting in a Shared Working Environment, *Proceedings of CSCW'92 Conference*, Turner, J. and Kraut, R. (Eds), The Association for Computing Machinery, New York, NY.

Rose, M. (1998), Germany's SAP Posts 72% Jump In Pretax Profit, *Wall Street Journal*, January 28.

Roskelly, H. (1994), The Risky Business of Group Work, *The Writing Teacher's Sourcebook*, Tate, G., Corbett, E. and Myers, N. (Eds), Oxford University Press, New York, NY.

Ruddell, S and Stevens, J.A. (1998), The Adoption of ISO 9000, ISO 14001, and The Demand for Certified Wood Products in The Business and Institutional Furniture Industry, V.48, No.3.

Russel, S. and Norvig, P. (1995), *Artificial Intelligence: A Modern Approach*, Prentice Hall, Upper Saddle River, NJ.

Senge, P.M. (1990), *The Fifth Discipline*, Doubleday, New York, NY.

Senge, P.M., Roberts, C., Ross, R.B., Smith, B.J. and Kleiner, A. (1994), *The Fifth Discipline Fieldbook*, Nicholas Brealey, London, UK.

Schmidt, K. (1994), *Modes and Mechanisms of Interaction in Cooperative Work*, Risø National Laboratory, Roskilde, Denmark.

Sheffield, J. and Gallupe, B. (1993), Using Electronic Meeting Technology to Support Economic Development in New Zealand: Short Term Results, *Journal of Management Information Systems*, V.10, No.3.

Simon, H.A. and Chase, W.G. (1973), Skill in Chess, *American Scientist*, V.61, No.4.

Smith, A. (1910), *The Wealth of Nations*, Vol.1, J.M. Dent & Sons, London, England (first published 1776).

Smith, A. (1910a), *The Wealth of Nations*, Vol.2, J.M. Dent & Sons, London, England (first published 1776).

Somerville, I. (1992), *Software Engineering*, Addison-Wesley, New York, NY.

Spender, J.C. (1996), Competitive Advantage from Tacit Knowledge? Unpacking the Concept and its Strategic Implications, *Organizational Learning and Competitive Advantage*, Moingeon, B. and Edmonson, A. (Eds), Sage, Thousand Oaks, CA.

Sproull, L. and Kiesler, S. (1986), Reducing Social Context Cues: Electronic Mail in Organizational Communication, *Management Science*, V.32, No.1.

Sproull, L. and Kiesler, S. (1991), Computers, Networks and Work, *Scientific American*, V.265, No.3.

Stacey, R.D. (1995), The Science of Complexity: An Alternative Perspective for Strategic Change Processes, *Strategic Management Journal*, V.16.

Strassmann, P. (1996), *The Value of Computers, Information and Knowledge*, Working paper, Strassmann Inc., New Canaan, CT.

Strassmann, P. (1997), *The Squandered Computer*, The Information Economics Press, New Canaan, CT.

Taylor, F.W. (1885), *A Piece Rate System*, McGraw-Hill, New York, NY.

Taylor, F.W. (1911), *The Principles of Scientific Management*, Norton & Company, New York, NY.

Teichman, J. and Evans, K.C. (1995), *Philosophy: A Beginner's Guide*, Blackwell, Oxford, UK.

Thomas, D. (1989), What's in an Object, *Byte*, March.

Toffler, A. (1970), *Future Shock*, Bantam Books, New York, NY.

Toffler, A. (1991), *Powershift*, Bantam Books, New York, NY.

Umar, A. (1997), *Object-Oriented Client/Server Internet Environments*, Prentice Hall, Upper Saddle River, NJ.

Venkatraman, N. (1994), IT-Enabled Business Transformation: From Automation to Business Scope Redefinition, *Sloan Management Review*, V.35, No.2.

Vennix, J.A.M. (1996), *Group Model Building: Facilitating Team Learning Using System Dynamics*, John Wiley & Sons, Chichester, England.

Walton, M. (1989), *The Deming Management Method*, Mercury, London.

Walton, M. (1991), *Deming Management at Work*, Mercury, London.

Ward P.T. and Mellor, S.J. (1985), *Structured Development for Real-Time Systems*, Yourdon Press, New York, N.Y.

Wastell, D.G., White, P. and Kawalek, P. (1994), A Methodology for Business Process Redesign: Experiences and Issues, *Journal of Strategic Information Systems*, 3(1).

Weick, K:E. and Bougon, M.G. (1986). *Organizations as Cognitive Maps: Charting Ways to Success and Failure, The Thinking Organizations*, Sims Jr., H.P. and Gioia, D.A. (Eds.), Jossey-Bass, San Francisco, CA.

Wensley, A. (1996). Book Review: Reengineering Mangement, *Business Change and Re-engineering*, 2(3).

White, T.E. and Fischer, L. (Eds.) (1994), *The Workflow Paradigm, Future Strategies*, Alameda, CA.

Woofford, J.C. (1994). Getting Inside the Leader's Head: A Cognitive Processes Approach to Leadership, *SAM Advanced Management Journal*, 59(3).

Yellen, R.E., Winniford, M. and Sandord, C.C. (1995). Extraversion and Intraversion in Electronically-Supported Meetings, Information & Management 28(1).

Yourdon, E. and Constantine, L.L. (1978). *Structured Design: Fundamentals of a Discipline of Computer Program and Systems Design*, Yourdon Press, New York, NY.

Zuboff, S. (1988). *In the Age of the Smart Machine: The Future of Work and Power*, Basic Books, New York, NY.

Zuboff, S. (1996). *The Abstraction of Industrial Work, Knowledge Mangement and Organizational Design*, Myers, P.S. (Ed.), Butterworth-Heinemann, Boston, MA.

Index

About the Author

Nereu (Ned) Florencio Kock, Jr. is a professor of management information systems of the Department of Computer and Information Sciences, Temple University, Philadelphia, PA. He holds a B.E.E. in electronics engineering from the Federal Center of Technological Education at Curitiba, Brazil, a M.Sc. in computer science from the Institute of Aeronautical Technology, Brazil, and a Ph.D. in information systems from the School of Management Studies, University of Waikato, New Zealand. Ned has been working as a systems analyst and management consultant since 1987, having been involved in projects at a number of organizations including Price Waterhouse, Johnson & Johnson, Rio de Janeiro State Construction Company, Westaflex, and the New Zealand Ministry of Agriculture and Fisheries. He is the author of the book *Process Re-engineering, PROI: A Practical Methodology,* published in Brazil by Vozes, and recipient of the MCB Press Outstanding Paper Award in 1997 in York, England. Ned has published over forty papers in international conferences and journals such as *Communications of the ACM, Journal of Organizational Computing and Electronic Commerce, Information & Management, Information Systems Journal,* and *Information Technology & People.*